I0814484

A History of Women in Piracy

Life Under the Black Flag

A History of Women in Piracy

Life Under the Black Flag

Roxanne Gregory

First published in Great Britain in 2025 by
Pen & Sword History
An imprint of
Pen & Sword Books Ltd
Yorkshire - Philadelphia

ISBN 978 1 39903 365 7

A CIP catalogue record for this book is available from the British Library.

Typeset in INDIA by IMPEC eSolutions
Printed and bound in England by CPI Group (UK) Ltd, Croydon, CRO 4YY

The Publisher's authorised representative in the EU for product safety is Authorised Rep Compliance Ltd., Ground Floor, 71 Lower Baggot Street, Dublin D02 P593, Ireland.
www.arccompliance.com

For a complete list of Pen & Sword titles please contact:

PEN & SWORD BOOKS LIMITED
George House, Units 12 & 13, Beevor Street, Off Pontefract Road,
Barnsley, S71 1HN, UK
E-mail: enquiries@pen-and-sword.co.uk
Website: www.pen-and-sword.co.uk

or

PEN AND SWORD BOOKS
1950 Lawrence Rd, Havertown, PA 19083, USA
E-mail: uspen-and-sword@casematepublishers.com
Website: www.penandswordbooks.com

Death leaves a heartache no one can heal.
Love leaves a memory no one can steal.
Forever young, always loved, my Viking son Matthew.

Special thanks to my family,
and to Amy Jordan and Lori Jones at Pen & Sword for their patience.

Contents

Glossary of Terms

Aetolians:	Confederation of tribal communities based in Aetolia in ancient Greece
Achaeans:	Greeks
Ardiaei:	Illyrian people who resided in modern-day Bosnia and Herzegovina
Arawaks:	Native people from the Caribbean and South America
Berbers:	Native people from North Africa
Brethren:	Comrades. Brethren of the Coast; a confederation of Caribbean pirates
Boucans:	Wooden equipment used to smoke meat
Boyar:	Highest-ranking member of the feudal nobility
Carthaginians:	A group of people originating from Phoenician settlers in North Africa, particularly around the city of Carthage
Corsairs:	Privateers and pirates
Dalmatia:	An historical region in modern-day Croatia and Montenegro
Dalmatians:	A group of Illyrian tribes in Dalmatia
Epirotes:	The inhabitants of Eprius
Epirus:	An historical region in southeastern Europe, now shared between Albania and Greece
Factors:	Managers
Fee farm:	Landholding, 'fee' being short for the word fiefdom
Gauls:	A group of Celtic people who inhabited a region in western Europe called Gaul
Grog or tot:	Alcohol
Hongs:	Chinese merchants
Illyria:	An historical region in the western Balkan Peninsula inhabited by Illyrians

Illyrians:	A group of people who resided in the western Balkan Peninsula during ancient times
Illyricum:	A province in southeastern Europe, mainly modern-day Croatia, Slovenia and northern Albania
Lalla:	Lady
Legionary *Legates*:	An ancient Roman general usually in charge of multiple legions and a province or territory
Letter of marque:	Government license
Lombards:	Cannons
Man-of-war:	Powerful warship
Matelotage:	A seventeenth-century equivalency to same-sex marriage
Phoenicians:	A powerful ancient Mediterranean maritime, trading people residing in city-states along the ancient coast of North Africa's Carthage and what is today Lebanon, Syria, and Cyprus
Piraguas	Small fishing canoes made from hollowed logs
Privateers	Pirate hunters
Pyrates:	Pirates
Quarter:	To capture a person or ship's crew rather than immediately kill them
Quick with child:	Pregnant
Strike the colours:	A demand to lower a ship's flag, a universal recognition of a surrender
Taíno:	Native people who were *Arawak* speaking
Tanka:	Native people from southern China
Tartane:	A small Mediterranean sailing ship with lateen sails
Tánaiste:	Heir apparent
Teredos:	Ship worm
Thracians:	An ancient group of people who inhabited southeastern Europe, modern-day Bulgaria, Romania, Turkey, northern Greece and northern Macedonia
Vizier:	A high official

Introduction

A History of Women in Piracy is a series of gripping, short biographies chronicling the lives and loves of daring women who flaunted convention and were every bit as capable as their male brethren who plied the high seas – some would say these women were even more capable pirates.

When you read the word 'pirates' most people think of the *Pirates of the Caribbean* film series or *Black Sails*, the small screen series, but the world of piracy has centuries-long history that is filled with little-known women who wielded real power in a 'man's' world long before they could vote in democratic elections.

Their stories are compelling and encompass women of all ethnicities and cultures. From Sayidda al-Hurra, Queen of the Barbary Pirates, a Muslim woman who successfully preyed on the shipping of her enemies and became governor of Tétouan in Morocco, to Zhèng Shì, an outlawed Tanka woman born in a brothel who rose to successfully command 17,000 men in the Red Flag Fleet, which at the time out rivalled the number of ships in the Imperial Chinese Navy.

During the Golden Age of Piracy (the period from 1650 to 1720), some women joined pirate crews even though the presence of a woman aboard ships often meant death, especially among the men who were the Brethren of the Coast – a coalition of pirates. At the time, many pirates considered women to be nothing more than inconvenient cargo or harbingers of ill luck.

Throughout history women pirates have used their wisdom and their wiles to outwit the men who pursued them. They were brave, intelligent, daring and determined women who fought with shields and swords, cutlasses and pistols as bravely – and sometimes more bravely – than their crews. Regardless of how they died, they lived as brave, resourceful women who defied the cultures of their times.

Chapter 1

Anne Bonny and The Republic of Pirates

Pirate:	Anne Bonny
Birth name:	Anne McCormac
Also known as:	Andy
	Anne Bonney
	Anne Bonnand
	Ann/Anne Fulford
	(and possibly also known as Annebelle, Annabelle and Ann Bonny)
Date of birth:	8 March 1697
Place of birth:	Kinsale, Ireland
Married:	James 'Jim' Bonny and Captain John 'Calico Jack' Rackham
Date of death:	April 1782?
Place of death:	Unknown
Ship:	*William*

'If you had fought like a man, you need not have been hanged like a dog',[1] said Anne Bonny as she met with her lover, pirate Captain John 'Calico Jack' Rackham, on the eve of his execution in St Jago de la Vega (Spanish Town), Jamaica in 1720. Both Bonny and Rackham were incarcerated having been captured, imprisoned, tried and condemned after a failed skirmish with English pirate hunter Captain Jonathan Barnet.[2]

On 22 October 1720, Rackham and his eighteen-'man' crew were aboard the twelve-gun sloop of war *William*, anchored in Discovery Bay (known locally as Dry Harbour Bay), near Negril Point on the leeward (western) side of Jamaica. The crew were liberally celebrating their latest skirmish as they had roundly trounced privateer Jean Bonadvis – who was originally from France – when Barnet's ship *Snow-Tygr* – a square-rigged merchantman with a dozen British Army troops and Royal Navy sailors – sailed into view. *William* also had in tow the sloop *The Mary and Sarah*, which Rackham and his crew had captured from Master Thomas Dillion.

The high season for vicious 'ship-killing' storms that plagued the Caribbean islands and wrecked countless ships of all flags, sending scores of seamen to their makers, was just beginning to ebb and by this mid-October night the seas had calmed. It was just before midnight, and the sea and skies were dark, but Rackham and his inebriated crew appeared unfazed and fearless.

Everyone aboard Rackham's vessel was sloshed. They had all been drinking gunpowder rum, a potent brew designed to keep barrelled water stores on board purified and the crew in high spirits. At the time, the British Royal Navy gave rum rations every day to all sailors, a practice that the Royal Navy would only discontinue in 1970.

A ration of 'grog or tot' as they called it was generally mixed with water and herbs to enhance the flavour.[3] A legacy of colonial Jamaica's vast sugarcane plantations, Royal Navy rum, at the time, was strong – 54 per cent pure alcohol, enough to give any career navy man cirrhosis by the time his service ended if pirates, hostile natives, warring enemies or their own officers did not kill him first.

Barnet was a privateer – an ex-pirate and current pirate bounty hunter for the governor of Jamaica, Sir Nicholas Lawes. Articled by the Crown's authority, Barnet hailed *William*: 'Who are you and where are you bound?'

Across the bay a drunken voice echoed in the night, 'John Rackham out of Cuba'.[4] Barnet boomed, 'In the name of the King of England, strike your colours …'[5]

Rackham and his crew refused, swearing, 'We will strike no strikes'[6] and fired a swivel gun at Barnet, who weighed the odds. *William* had twelve guns, but what Barnet did not know was that the ship had no cannon balls left as the crew had expended these during their previous skirmish with Bonadvis.

British vessels like the *Snow-Tygr* were not equipped at the time with standard artillery guns or ordnance rounds, so Barnet would have used cannon balls weighing anywhere from 4 to 32 pounds to bring down Rackham's boom and disable his ship.[7]

Without further warning, Barnet's gunners turned their deck swivel guns on *William*, sweeping the foredeck with murderous fire. Then Barnet ordered his gunners to fire the lombards. A cannon ball pierced *William*'s side and started a fire in the hold, while another struck the ship's boom and it collapsed. Under a hail of fire, Rackham and all but two of his crew descended into the hold, allegedly to try and extinguish the fire.

The two crew 'men' left atop were armed to the teeth with pistols, cutlasses and boarding axes, which they wielded with Banshee-like fury, as Barnet's crew grappled *William* and began boarding.

The crew members were astonished to discover the two screaming Banshees on deck were not men, but women: Anne Bonny and Mary Read. Both women fought like tigers.

At one point, Read was so disgusted with the men who stayed below deck that she stopped fighting and raced to the hold crying, 'If there's a man among ye, ye'll come up and fight like the man ye are to be!' When the men refused, she fired a shot into the hold, wounding one crewman.[8]

Rackham's crew begged for quarter, so that the crew would be captured and not immediately killed, it was a call for surrender. Barnet's crew eventually overpowered the two women and clapped them in irons before marching Rackham and the rest of his crew from the hold.

They were transported to Davis Cove, near Lucea in Jamaica and turned over to Major Richard James, a militia officer,[9] who took them into custody to await a swift and speedy trial.

Taken to Spanish Town on the island of Jamaica for trial, the magistrate realised that two women were among the pirates and, thus, their trials were ordered to be held separately from the men.

On 16 November 1720, in Spanish Town, Rackham and his crew – except Bonny and Read – were tried for numerous crimes. Brought before the bar, in their defence they pleaded 'not guilty', saying that they only plundered Spanish ships, not English ones, but they offered nothing of 'substance' in their defence and they were found guilty. The magistrate donned his black cap and passed the sentence:

> You John Rackham, George Fetherston, Richard Corner, John Davies, John Howell, Patrick Carty, Thomas Earl, James Dobbin and Noah Harwood, are to go from hence to the place from whence you came [the gaol] and thence from the place to Execution; where you shall be

> severally hanged by the Neck, until you are severally dead. And God of his infinite Mercy be merciful to every one of your souls.[10]

Rackham and his crew were executed shortly after their trial; no appeals were permitted. Friday, 18 November 1720 dawned humid, overcast and gloomy when Rackham, Fetherston, Corner, Davies and Howell were hanged at Gallows Point in Port Royal, near Kingston.

Harwood, Dobbin, Carty and Earl were executed the following day in Kingston. Other crewmen Thomas Brown and John Fenwick were executed the following Monday in Port Royal.

As ringleaders, the bodies of Rackham, Fetherston and Corner were afterward hung inside on gibbets with chains and displayed at three different locations as 'an example to the public', where they would remain until their bodies decayed.[11] Rackham's body was even tarred, being hung in what is today known as Rackham's Cay.

Both Bonny and Read pleaded 'not guilty'[12] before the assize. At their trial on 28 November 1720, Bonny was eloquent, unrepentant and oft times defiant throughout the proceedings.

Testifying for the prosecution, two French sailors who had been aboard *The Mary and Sarah* – the sloop that Rackham and his crew had taken earlier in October 1720 – swore that the women

> Were very active on board and willing to do Any Thing. That Ann[e] Bonny, the prisoner at the bar, handed gun-powder to the men. That when they saw any vessel, gave chase or attacked, they [Bonny and Read] wore Men's Cloath's [*sic*]; and at other times they wore Women's Cloath's; [*sic*] That they did not seem to be kept, or de'tained [*sic*] by force, but of their Own Free Will and Consent.[13]

Thomas Dillion of *The Mary and Sarah* recounted that after he and his crew surrendered to Rackham, they were advised to come aboard *William* while their ship was plundered, where they discovered Bonny and Read dressed as men in 'short coats and trousers with kerchiefs tied round their heads and long hair' and Bonny was holding a pistol.

Dillon swore that 'They [Bonny and Read] were both very profligate, cursing and swearing much, and very ready and willing to do Any Thing on board'.[14]

When asked by the magistrate if they had any witnesses who could offer their relief, both Bonny and Read said 'no', nor did they have any defence of the charges. A short recess ensued, but afterward they were both found guilty and sentenced to death. After their sentencing, they asked the court if their sentences might be stayed as they were both 'quick with child'.[15]

English law at the time forbade the execution of a pregnant woman regardless of her crimes as the unborn baby was innocent and deserving of life, even as an orphan. The magistrate ordered their sentences to be reprised until examinations could be made and the court was adjourned until 19 December 1720. Both women were, in fact, with child and had their sentences staid, but as soon as their babies were born, Read and Bonny would be taken to the gallows for execution.

***

'Twenty-three years earlier [on 8 January 1697], William McCormac [also known as McCormack and later Cormac] begrudgingly added his name and a small tithe to the subscription being solicited about for the restoration of the Church at Kinsale, Ireland.'[16]

McCormac was struggling to make his law practice flourish when, on 8 March 1697 (some people believe that the year may have been later), his servant, Mary Brennan, gave birth to his bastard child, a fiery-haired baby girl. They chose to name the baby Anne – after Princess Anne, a Protestant who had married Prince George, heir to the Crown of Denmark.

McCormac and Brennan were much in love, a chronic affront and pain to his aristocratic wife who lived in Cobh (it would have been known by Queenstown at the time), in Cork Harbour, who had turned Brennan out of the house when she discovered McCormac's infidelities with her. McCormac's wife had Brennan arrested for 'bedding'[17] a married man, but she was released when it was proved she was pregnant with his child.

Furthermore, to add insult to injury, McCormac's wife had demanded that he live elsewhere, although to keep up appearances and avoid a scandal that would forever tarnish them both, she would allow him a monthly allowance as he set up his law practice.

Little did she know that McCormac had taken Brennan with him to begin a new life in Kinsale, Ireland now a prosperous corporation and growing port town that victualled Britain's Royal Navy, and the homeward bound West Indies Fleet.[18]

That year, the erstwhile fathers of the Corporation of Kinsale had enacted rather stringent new laws against all manner of offences. Blaspheming now became a constant source of revenue, and if the blasphemer could not come up with a shilling a day, in 'the cage' would suffice. The ducking stool had also been repaired and was ready for use with scolds and bawds.[19] McCormac's practice might benefit from minor criminal prosecutions, but maritime tort law was his bread and butter. While British trade with the West Indies and the slave trade with the Canary Islands made Kinsale prosper, French privateers ruthlessly raided Irish ports.

George Fort in Kinsale featured a British garrison whose soldiers were paid poor wages of 2 shillings a month. They depended on the Irish fishing fleet for much of their sustenance and, although initially protected by the governor, recently the Royal Navy had impressed – and scared – members of the fishing fleet, and the Irish fishermen were fearful of being out on the water or in the streets. Town fathers fretted that the soldiers would starve or desert.[20] The Corporation of Old Kinsale's barristers, with no access to an Admiralty court, took their cases to London.

It was not long after Anne's birth that McCormac, Brennan and baby Anne (Bonny) moved to London to ply his maritime barrister's trade.

In the early 1700s, London was exploding with maritime wealth, brought by the slave trade and the exploitation of the Americas and West Indies. There was work aplenty for McCormac in London, but he also ran the risk of running into his wife's family as she had relatives in the city.

In order to hide his illegitimate daughter from them, he had her hair cut and dressed her as a boy. By the age of 10, she was working in his law office and given the name Andy.[21] Known as McCormac's ward, she was soon to become his clerk, but when his wife's family discovered Brennan at his residence and Andy's ruse, McCormac's wife precipitously cut off his allowance.

Like Sir Issac Newton who had invested £20,000 (approximately $1,530,785.71 in today's money) in the South Sea Company, McCormac also speculated in stocks and made a number of investments. Akin to the Hudson's Bay Company, the governors of the company were keen to ruthlessly exploit the Americas, despite the Spanish having a firm grip on the South American continent. Even the English king and his two mistresses were heavily invested in South Sea Company stock, which King George I (1660–1727) affectionately called 'his child'.[22]

By 1720, speculation had pushed the price of a single South Sea Company share to £1,000 (which would be worth much more in today's money).[23] Then the company suffered a mysterious disaster. More of a Ponzi scheme than an actual explorations company, the South Sea Company bubble burst and hundreds of London's fair and finest were financially ruined.

Heads rolled for fraud, and skirting debtor's prison, McCormac decided he would try his luck as a barrister in the British colonial province called the Providence of Carolina (part of the modern-day United States of America).

Bonny was not amused. She had a short fuse and did not take her transition from up-and-coming law clerk to colonial barrister's daughter in her stride. She was wilful and disobedient. At 13, shortly after her mother died of typhoid fever, 'in her passion' she stabbed and severely wounded a local servant girl with a kitchen knife. Described as being 'of a fierce and courageous temper',[24] Bonny was a rebellious child.

She did not care for provincial life in the Carolinas, nor for her father's plans for her future. Although McCormac failed to prosper as a barrister, his former connections with the South Sea Company opened provincial business offers for him, and his knowledge of maritime law assisted him as a merchant. He changed his surname to Cormac, as to better blend with the provincial detritus of empire.[25]

In three short years, he had amassed a small fortune and a sizable plantation outside Charles Town (as it was known at that time), making Bonny a potentially wealthy catch. An attractive 'slip of a girl' with fiery-red hair and green eyes, Bonny was surrounded by suitors. She reportedly 'beat the socks off' one potential husband who attempted to rape her. In her rage, she was reputed to have beaten the man so viciously that 'he lay ill [for] a considerable time.'[26]

It was not long after that Bonny met her future husband, James 'Jim' Bonny, who was, by all accounts, an unscrupulous brigand, given to petty piracy. James wanted to marry Anne for her future inheritance.

Horrified, McCormac forbade their relationship, but his daughter defied him and they married anyway. McCormac promptly disinherited his daughter, banishing her from his home. Bonny would have been an heiress had she not defiantly married a penniless pirate or, as author Captain Charles Johnson puts it, 'a young fellow who belonged to the sea, and was not worth a Groat'.[27]

James Bonny and his new wife set sail for New Providence Island in The Bahamas, then on to James's home, the Pirates' Republic – a place run by privateers turned pirates. Desperate for cash as he had not been a very successful pirate, in 1718 (before he met Anne) in Nassau in The Bahamas, James Bonny took the king's pardon, an official amnesty offered to pirates by the Crown. He had been engaged in petty piracy and worked as a piratical informer for former privateer governor Woodes Rogers, The Bahamas' new lord proprietor, who was determined to offer the king's pardon to pirates, and if that failed, Rogers planned to exterminate piracy in the Caribbean.

Drunk one night in a New Providence Island tavern, James Bonny began beating his wife – it appears that this may have been a regular occurrence as James had no affection for Anne, he had only married her for her future inheritance. John 'Calico Jack' Rackham intervened and stopped the beating.

Born in Jamaica in 1682, Rackham, a renowned ladies' man, much given to wearing colourful clothing, had been celebrated pirate Charles Vane's quartermaster before he also took the king's pardon and tuned on Vane, hunting him as a privateer. Called 'Calico Jack' because he eschewed the silks favoured by other pirates and wore cottons instead, Rackham offered to buy Anne from James, a common practice at the time, but James refused.[28]

Fifteen years her senior, Rackham decided to woo Anne instead with baubles, gold and jewels. She was smitten with her 'rogue gentleman' and left her husband.

It was not long before James Bonny complained to Woodes Rogers and Rogers ordered Anne, who was then pregnant by Rackham, to return to her husband or face the lash publicly for her infidelity.[29] Some claim Rogers swore he would force Rackham to wield the lash![30]

Rackham again asked James Bonny if he would part with Anne and consent to an annulment of his marriage. Avariciously, James suggested a sizable sum,[31] which Rackham agreed to, but James wanted the transaction witnessed and so he chose Richard Turnley, a much-despised man who had assisted Rogers's entry into Nassau.

Believing marriage was for life, Turnley went directly to Rogers and told him about the scheme and Rogers made Anne promise, on pain of flogging, that she would return to her husband. Now heavily pregnant with Rackham's child, Anne had no intention of returning to him.

Rackham, having taken the king's pardon, was living off the avails of his last score: bolts of silk and fine laces. However, working for the king was not to Rackham's liking and he decided his best chance at saving Anne was to steal a ship and return to the pirate trade with her.

Once again Rackham raised his flag, the Jolly Roger, stealing several vessels before deciding to hijack a ship, *Curlew* (also known as *William*), on 22 August 1720. *William* was a twelve-gun sloop of war, which was at that time one of the fastest ships afloat, belonging to privateer John 'Catch Him If You Can' Ham.[32]

Despite being heavily pregnant, Anne Bonny, with her friend Mary Read, whom she met, not at sea as claimed in *A General History of the Pyrates*,[33] but in the inns of New Providence Island, together with Rackham and a handful of others boarded *William* with pistols at the ready.

Dressed as a sailor, Bonny threatened to blow the brains out of the men who were on watch while Rackham and the other crew members took *William* by force.[34] They succeeded in overcoming Ham's crew and Rackham's crew voted for him to become captain of *William*.

However, while leaving the harbour they were challenged by Woodes Rogers's watch aboard the ship *Delica*. Smoothly, and to avoid suspicion, Rackham explained they were going to 'stand outside the harbour for the night'[35] as they had lost an anchor chain. Instead, they circled round the back of New Providence Island and began plundering piraguas – small fishing canoes – and other maritime craft, many that were simply fishing.

A witness, fisherwoman Dorothy Thomas, later testified that she had been fishing in one of the canoes when Rackham and his crew stole her fish and gear. She stated that Bonny and Read, 'wore long trousers and men's jackets and had kerchiefs wrapped round their heads … a pistol and machete in their hands … They cursed and swore at the men, urging them that they should kill me to prevent my testifying against them.'[36]

Not only did Bonny and Read wield cutlasses, machetes, boarding axes and pistols, they frequently brought gunpowder and cannon balls to the gunners.

Rackham and his crew were also on the hunt for Turnley whom they knew was hunting turtles on one of The Bahamas outer cays. After a couple of weeks, they found his ship. Managing to impress three of his crew, they were able to sink his vessel, while Turnley and his son hid for their lives in the nearby woods. Rackham and Bonny left a fourth member of Turnley's crew ashore with a warning that if they ever found him, they would flog Turnley to death.[37]

Rackham and his crew then set sail for Cuba, where Bonny gave birth to a son (some accounts claim a daughter). It is supposed that Bonny left the child with a friend of Rackham's, but other accounts report that the child was stillborn.

Rackham was unusual in having fighting women aboard his vessel. Among the Brethren of the Coast, a crewman could be killed for harbouring a woman on board, while others had strict rules about hijacking passengers who were women. 'If at any time we meet with a prudent woman, that man that offers to meddle with her without her consent, shall suffer present death',[38] claimed Captain John Phillips of the ship *Revenge*. While other pirates simply dumped all women overboard as inconvenient cargo.

Lower-class women and slaves, however, were wrongly seen as inferior and would have been considered 'fair game'. At the time, men would have had no respect for women and while sailing as a privateer, Woodes Rogers, apparently delivered a parson to a remote locale and is said to have 'set him ashore with the prettiest … slave'. One would have hoped that a religious man would have had more of a moral compass, but this was probably not the case, and Rogers was sure the reverend would 'crack a few commandments with [the slave]'.[39]

Between September and the end of October 1720, and aboard *William*, Rackham, Bonny and Read terrorised shipping between Jamaica, Cuba, Saint Domingue and The Bahamas to the point where Rogers and the governor of Jamaica sent several privateers scouring the cays and bays after them. Jean Bonadvis caught up with Rackham on the western edge of Jamaica while he was recruiting new crew members.

Rather than trying to evade Bonadvis, Rackham opened fire on his ship. Bonadvis was outgunned and he knew it. Under withering cannon fire, he beat a hasty retreat and notified Jonathan Barnet who had also been searching for Rackham. Barnet and his crew subsequently boarded *William* and captured Rackham and his crew, who were thereafter tried, found guilty and sentenced to death.

A few months after the trial, Read was reported to have died from 'white fever', but some claim she died in childbirth while still imprisoned. She was buried at St Catherine's Church in Jamaica.

Miraculously, Bonny escaped the gallows. Some sources claim her wealthy father offered a bribe for her release, and she returned to his plantation outside Charles Town with her child. There it was reported she changed her name to Annebelle or Annabelle, married Joseph Burleigh, a Jamaican civil servant, and had eight children, dying in her bed at the ripe old age of 88.[40]

Historian Nigel Cawthorne claims that Bonny was ransomed by her father and became the mistress of former Red Sea pirate Robert Fenwick, who lived with her at Fenwick Castle outside of Charles Town. Cawthorne relates that she ran away from Fenwick with a younger lover, but they were caught, and Bonny was forced to help Fenwick hang her lover.

Others maintain that Bonny married a plantation owner and settled in Tidewater, Virginia, where she became a grandmother, possibly a great-grandmother, and died in her bed in her mid-eighties in April 1782.

However, the parish records for St Catherine's Church in Jamaica – where Mary Read was buried – list the death of woman named Ann Bonny on 29 December 1733.

What actually happened to Anne Bonny is unknown, but she is one of the most well-known pirates – particularly as she was a woman. So well-remembered, in fact, that many subsequent films have been based on the life of Anne Bonny.

Chapter 2

Mary Read, Three's Company

Pirate:	**Mary Read**
Also known as:	**Mary Reade**
Date of birth:	**1685**
Place of birth:	**London, England**
Married:	**Twice married but the names of the husbands are unknown**
Date of death:	**? April 1721**
Place of death:	**Port Royal, Jamaica**
Ship:	***William***

Mary Read was a remarkable person, who lived most of her life not as a woman but as a man. But Read had never intended to become a pirate. For many years she had fought as a soldier and able seaman in foreign wars for her king and country.

According to Nigel Cawthorne in his book, *A History of Pirates Blood and Thunder on the High Seas*,[1] after Anne Bonny gave birth to John 'Calico Jack' Rackham's child in Cuba, leaving their child for safekeeping there, Rackham and his crew took a Dutch ship where they forced some of the crew to accept pirate articles and join them. In Cawthorne's account, Bonny was attracted to a good-looking Dutch 'boy': Read, who revealed her gender to Bonny and the two became lovers. However, Rackham raged with jealousy, threatening to slice Read's throat, until she revealed her breasts, which were 'quite white'. Not only was Read a woman, she was not Dutch either, but English.

Read's early years and date of birth are shrouded in mystery. However, what is known is that her mother, living in an English port town married a sailor and became pregnant by him, but he disappeared at sea.[2] Read's mother petitioned her husband's mother (her mother-in-law) for support for the child who was born a boy, but she soon became pregnant with another man's child, so she went to live in the countryside where she gave birth to Read in 1685. On her return her son sadly died.

Unable to live without her mother-in-law's financial allowance for the child, she substituted Read for the boy and dressed her as such. A successful deception that lasted more than a decade.

At 13, Read was made a foot boy in service of an aristocratic house. Later, she was recommended by them and signed on with a British naval vessel as a cabin boy. For several years she served as a crewman aboard a British man-of-war.

When war ended, Read left England and joined the Dutch military, serving with distinction as a dragoon infantryman in Flanders during the Spanish War of Succession. While serving she was struck by cupid's arrow and her Flemish tent mate insisted they marry, much to the surprise and support of their fellows.

Some historians claim both soldiers retired with their military pensions and with gifts from supportive brother-in-arms, they opened an inn – The Three Horseshoes – near Breda Castle in the Netherlands. For the first time in her life, as an innkeeper and dutiful wife, Read wore women's clothing, but their happy-ever-after nuptials were not to last, as her husband died suddenly less than two years later.

Read cut her hair and donned her trousers once again and tried to rejoin the military, but with the war ended there was not much opportunity for advancement, and so she left and boarded a ship bound for the New World's adventure in the West Indies.

Colin Woodward in his seminal work, *The Republic of Pirates Being the True and Surprising Story of the Caribbean Pirates and The Man Who Brought Them Down*,[3] claims Rackham, Bonny and Read did not meet at sea but in one of the inns in Nassau, where she agreed to join their crew. Woodward posits that, at the time, Read and Bonny's gender was well-known as they were described as 'pirate women' in a Boston newspaper article by soon-to-be governor Woodes Rogers. What is known is that the three enjoyed intimate company until Read fell for another of Rackham's crewman and actually married him. She was carrying a child when they were imprisoned.

Read and Bonny were tried and convicted on 28 November 1720; the court reconvened in December 1720, and their pregnant states were attested to and they were returned to the Spanish Town goal to await the birth of their babies.

According to parish records, Read contracted a virulent 'white fever' (smallpox) and died while incarcerated. She was buried at St Catherine's church in Jamaica on 28 April 1721. There does not appear to be any record of the birth of the child, so Read may have died before the baby was born.

Coincidentally perhaps, a virulent 'white fever' was initially thought to be brought by ship from the West Indies to Boston, Massachusetts in spring 1721. Devastating fever swept the city, infecting 5,759 people out of 10,600. Between April 1721 and February 1722, 844 people were recorded dead of the disease.

Mary Read is one of the most famous known pirates – especially the most well-known English woman pirate.

Chapter 3

Marie-Anne Dieu-le-Veut, God Willing

Pirate:	**Marie-Anne Dieu-le-Veut**
Also known as:	**Anne Dieu-le-Veut**
	Anne/Marie-Anne Chérel
	Anne/Marie-Anne Lelong
	(Dieu-le-Veut translates to God Willing or God Wills It)
Date of birth:	**28 August 1661**
Place of birth:	**Gourin Morbihan Brittany, France**
Married:	**Pierre Lelong**
	Joseph Chérel
	Laurens Cornelis Boudewijn de Graaf (also known as Lorencillo de Graaf)
Date of death:	**11 January 1710**
Place of death:	**Unknown**

In 1568, the Spanish governor of Rio de la Achí in New Spain (modern-day Mexico) complained bitterly to his King Phillip II:

> For every two ships coming here from Spain, there are twenty corsairs. For this reason, not a single city on this coast is safe because they seize and plunder settlements by their whim. They have become arrogant to such an extent that they call themselves rulers of land and sea.[1]

Marie-Anne Dieu-le-Veut must have cried tears of joy when finally, she reached dry land on the shores of Tortuga Island (or *Île de la Tortue* as it was known, which forms part of modern-day Haiti) in the Caribbean, sometime in the early 1670s. Born in Gourin Morbihan in Brittany, France in summer 1661, not much is known of Dieu-le-Veut's early life.

In the mid-sixteenth century there were two primary ways for a woman to establish a life in the Caribbean islands. In France, the French West India Company, incorporated as an adventure-capitalist concern, was granted by the Crown, the West Indies islands and French possessions along the Atlantic coasts of America and Africa. The company was also granted a monopoly on trade with America, for a term of forty years.

French West India Company factors were concerned that French possessions in the New World would be best served by colonists rather than single men, who at that time, made up most of the population within French-held lands.

Within the first month of their incorporation in 1664, they raised a fleet of forty-five ships to trade with the French possessions, now under their command and control. Speculation in French West India Company shares was brisk, almost riotous sometimes and the furore for those shares can only be compared with the rampant speculation in the historic Dutch tulip bulbs investment scheme of 1636, which saw anyone who was anyone buying shares in tulip bulb stocks.

But the company needed colonists, and they came up with innovative solutions. Their agents offered transportation to French colonies in exchange for a contracted indentured service of three and a half years. They preferred indenturing couples and while some historians claim that Dieu-le-Veut's daughter was born in France, if that is true, the most likely way she got to Tortuga Island was as an indentured servant. Other historians claim she landed on the shores of Tortuga Island as a former prisoner, most likely a freed sex worker offered 'transportation' in lieu of imprisonment.

The French West India Company was busy; tobacco was one of their biggest sellers and the inlands of Tortuga Island offered soil perfect for tobacco growing. But they were also shorthanded and while importing slaves was risky, expensive and possibly fatal if there was a slave up-rising, the company needed colonists. At the time almost 2,000 men, buccaneers, pirates and privateers called Tortuga Island home. They manned a variety of swift ships from fleet, single-sail corsairs to sloops and purloined man-of-wars.

Like the French West India Company, the French East India Company also needed colonists to fill company quotas, and in 1663 the company sent 800 imprisoned French sex workers, 'the King's Daughters', to North America to settle in New France (Quebec and the Canadian Martimes today). Only one of the 'King's Daughters', Catherine Guichelin, was subsequently recorded as having been charged with prostitution in New France after her husband left her.[2]

Tortuga Island had changed hands before the French established their colony, having previously been settled by both the Spanish and English. Sea turtles, a staple food of pirates and privateers, were in abundance there, and only 4 miles wide and 20 miles long, diminutive Tortuga Island, because of its strategic location, became a major outpost in the Caribbean Sea lanes and a den of debauchery by the 1600s.[3]

Three leagues off the northwestern coast of Hispañola – sometimes referred to as Hispaniola (today two nations – the Dominican Republic and Haiti) – at its zenith the island's strategic location attracted pirates and privateers who plotted, planned and intercepted Portuguese and Spanish treasure galleons heading toward the Spanish Main (the Spanish held territory in the Americas) through the Windward Passage.

Tortuga Island was home to the Brethren of the Coast, a loose French, English, Dutch and freed-slaves coalition of privateers and pirates, and Tortuga Island was the celebrated pirate capital of the Caribbean until Port Royal in Jamaica rose to fame as the 'The Wickedest City the New World.'[4] Before being devastated by an earthquake, Port Royal would also be called 'New Sodom' by others.

The Brethren of the Coast were governed by a pirate code and ships' articles – written contracts – that favoured democratic decision making, hierarchical command authority, individual rights and equitable division of spoils. Medical systems were in place with a ship's surgeon getting a larger share than a carpenter, and injured crewmen were invalidated with defined spoils. For example, if a man lost his arm in a skirmish, he would receive 600 pieces of eight, silver coins of common currency and more for a leg.

According to Alexander Exquemelin, a former buccaneer surgeon, who initially came to the Caribbean as an indentured servant, each pirate's roles and expectations in the articles a man signed were clearly defined. Exquemelin's tell-all book *De Americanensche Zee-Roovers* (American Sea Rovers also known as Buccaneers of America), first published in Amsterdam in 1678 is an inside look at buccaneers lives during the Golden Age of Piracy.

The Brethren of the Coast's Custom of the Coast (code of conduct) allowed them to elect a captain, second mate and quartermaster, agree on articles under which they sailed, and have shipboard meetings to decide where they were headed and for what – provisions or prizes. Candles and lanterns were to be put out at 8.00 pm, and weapons were to be clean and fit for service. There would be no desertion, no quarrelling and no stealing. The code also defined booty (no prey, no pay). Captains were elected by vote and they and the ship's owners received extra shares. The shipwright or carpenter had a fixed salary. Surgeons' salaries were capped, and the first pirate to locate or to board a prize won an extra share, whereas cabin boys received only half a share. Medical care was assured.

> For the loss of a right arm, 600 pieces of eight or six slaves; for the loss of a left arm, 500 pieces of eight or five slaves; for a right leg, 500 pieces of eight or five slaves; for the left leg, 400 pieces of eight or four slaves; for an eye, one-hundred pieces of eight or one slave; for a finger the same as for an eye. All is paid in common stock.[5]

Matelotage was acknowledged, wherein before his brothers, men exchanged gold rings and one man pledged himself to another, to share his life and spoils, and in the event of his death, to be buried by his mate. Among the buccaneers of Tortuga Island and the Brethren of the Coast, matelotage defined a sexual partner.[6]

According to B.R. Burg's seminal work in *Sodomy and the Pirate Tradition: English Sea Rovers in the Seventeenth-Century Caribbean*, second edition:[7]

> Aside from the production of children, homosexuals alone can fulfil [*sic*] satisfactorily all human needs, wants and desires, all the while supporting and sustaining a human community remarkable by the very fact that it is unremarkable … The male engaging in homosexual activity aboard a pirate ship in the West Indies three centuries past was simply an ordinary member of his community, completely socialized and acculturated.

The Brethren of the Coast regulated their privateering enterprises within the community of privateers, and with their outside benefactors, under the protection of a government license called a letter of marque and reprisal. Dutch, French, English and Spanish governors of all colonies issued letters of marque, legalising and legitimising piracy in the eyes of their respective crowns, especially during times of war.

The Brethren of the Coast arose from the small groups of buccaneer hunters who inhabited the Caribbean islands. Native Arawaks taught these hunters how to cure, smoke and dry the meat of pigs and cattle atop green-wood grates, called boucans. The French called these hunters *boucanier* or buccaneer in English.

Tortuga Island's buccaneers earned a good living selling logwood and pork and beef jerky, which turned dark red during the smoking process, and it kept for weeks. They also sold tallow, the fat rendered from bone marrow, used to make candles and as a preservative used in coating the hulls of wooden ships as a precaution against teredos, which would burrow into hulls leaving them weakened and looking like Swiss cheese.

Buccaneers in the bushlands lived in groups of six or eight agreeing to share all they had with one another. Some men lived together as committed couples. But they must have been fearsome to meet on the streets as they were invariably scarred and armed to the teeth with knives, matchlocks, pistols and cutlasses. Buccaneers living in the bushlands, apparently, seldom washed and slaughtering wild hogs and cattle is a dirty business as is gutting and smoking the meat.

> When they returned from the chase to the boucan, you would say that these are the butcher's vilest servants, who have been eight days in the slaughter-house without washing … As they frequently carried the meat home by cutting a hole in the centre, and thrusting their heads through it, we may imagine the cannibals that they must have looked. They wore drawers, or frequently only tight moccasins, reaching to the knee; their sandals were of bull's hide or hog skin, fastened with leather … they wore tunics, belted with a strip of green hide … Their tunics became coloured purple with the blood of wild cattle.[8]

Dieu-le-Veut arrived on the sandy shores of mountainous Tortuga Island, which lies north of Santo Domingo (in modern-day Dominican Republic, but which was known as Saint Domingue at the time). Pulling into a southern port, possibly at Cayona, she stepped ashore when resilient and resourceful Bertrand d'Ogeron de La Bouëre (1613–1676) was governor between 1665 and 1675.

Prior to d'Ogeron de La Bouëre's tenure, French engineer Jean le Vasseur had raided the island during the early 1640s, quickly taking control of the islands major ports and establishing himself as the governor. Le Vasseur is also credited with the construction of the Fort de la Rocher overlooking the island's main harbour. His fort bristled with forty cannon and was designed to deter further encroachments by the Spanish.

Alarmed by the lack of colonists and knowing Tortuga Island's population was mostly pirate men, le Vasseur imported 2,000 French sex workers from France's prisons with a promise of freedom and marriage.[9]

The official 'blind-eye' lawlessness under La Vasseur's governorship made Tortuga Island an enticing base for piracy to freely operate. Le Vasseur opened the port to privateers of all nations, in exchange for a toll, a percentage of the wealth of every vessel anchoring inside his waters.

His efforts at luring matelotage mates to live with women foundered, although history records a few instances of matelotage mates actually marrying women in order to share them. La Vasseur's attempt at luring men from plundering to farming met with dismal success.[10]

Tortuga Island was divided into four geographical areas at the time. The Low Lands or Low Country included most of the ports. The wealthiest plantation owners lived in Cayona, which featured fine villas. The middle planation lands were inland where there were vast plantations of tobacco. The western side of the island was known as La Ringot, while the mountainous northern section of the island was known as Le Montage.

During the slow hunting season, Tortuga Island's buccaneers turned to piracy and privateering. Operating canoes hollowed out from tree trunks, periaguas or single-sailed barques, they roved the sea with muskets instead of cannon, attacking under cover of night.

Single-masted sloops soon became the vessel of choice due to their manoeuvrability in shallow water. Sloops made in Bermuda were the fastest sloops of their kind. Big enough to allow for fifty-man crews and eleven to fourteen guns, they were swift on the water. Buccaneer numbers increased under le Vasseur and with that came success... until Spain intervened.

Tortuga Island's easily defended harbours, fresh water and sheltered anchorage attracted adventurers. Its prime location at the head of the Windward Passage provided a vantage point from which to spy and strike loaded Spanish treasure ships returning to Europe heavily laden with South American gold and silver or treasure from Asia.

Outraged their treasure-ship galleons were being looted, the Spanish retaliated. Returning to Tortuga Island in an attempt to depopulate it, they slaughtered all the pigs and cattle they could find, hoping to forever cripple Tortuga Island's economy. Ironically, with their livelihood dying, buccaneers were forced to make a living the only other way they knew how, by raiding.

Spanish lords, realising their mistake, tried to reverse the damage but every effort was repulsed. By this time, Tortuga Island had a life of its own. It had become a common place of refuge for all sorts of wickedness, a seminary of pirates and thieves.

We may never know whether Dieu-le-Veut came as a former sex worker or as an indentured servant, what we do know is that she was unlucky in love. In 1684, she married buccaneer Pierre Lelong and four years later they had a daughter, Marie Marguerite Yvonne Lelong (1688–1774). But two years later, in 1690, her husband was seriously injured and died during a fight, leaving Dieu-le-Veut a buccaneer widow.

Dieu-le-Veut found a new husband, Joseph Chérel, and they had married within a year of her first husband's death, marrying in 1691. They had a child and named him Jean-François Chérel (1692–1732), but Joseph Chérel died in June 1693, presumably by the hands of Laurens Cornelis Boudewijn de Graaf (also known as Lorencillo de Graaf), a celebrated and savvy Dutch pirate captain.

Now twice widowed, Dieu-le-Veut was with two small children and struggling to make ends meet. De Graaf was 'tall, blonde and handsome' with a Spanish-style moustache and was previously married to a woman from the Canary Islands called Petronilla Guzman.[11]

At the time, it was rumoured that de Graaf who was born in Dordrecht, Holland (the Netherlands) had come to the Caribbean, first as a gunner aboard a Spanish vessel, who was captured by buccaneers and when given the choice, he joined them, rising to become one of the most feared and most accomplished pirate captains ever to sail Caribbean seas. Although a terror to Spanish colonists who called him Diablo – the Devil – he kept musicians aboard his vessels and was 'known among filibusters by his courtesy and his good taste'.[12]

De Graaf also protected those he took hostage, ensuring their lives were saved, something that set him at cross purposes with other pirates of the day. In fact, when he and Nikolas van Hoorn were raiding Veracruz and took hostages, they waited on the little island of Los Sacrificos for the ransoms to be paid, but van Hoorn became restless and took the heads of several hostages sending them to the Spanish governor, while de Graaf was away. When de Graaf discovered the hostage deaths, he confronted van Hoorn, a renowned and very accomplished pirate, and requested a duel. The two men fought, and van Hoorn was sliced across his wrist, a wound that became gangrenous and within two weeks he had sepsis fever and died.

De Graaf prided himself on never taking a commission from any lord, governor or king, and would put into any port held by any nation without fear or favour. But in September 1683, he sent a letter to the governor of Jamaica, Sir Thomas Lynch offering his privateering services to the British. De Graaf was granted a pardon and a letter of marque. His pirating career and the prizes he took and the battles he won was nothing short of astonishing. De Graaf was a very accomplished captain and his raiding and taking of prizes was at its zenith when he walked into a woman seeking revenge.

Folk tradition has it that in March 1693, Dieu-le-Veut was drinking in a tavern possibly in Cayona or Basse-Terre on Tortuga Island when de Graaf and his crew jocularly walked inside. Defiantly Dieu-le-Veut challenged him to a duel as blood justice for the untimely death of her husband Joseph Chérel whom she alleged de Graaf had killed the year before. De Graaf was taken aback.

When she challenged him to a duel, the good-looking Dutchman laughed. But as he unsheathed his sword, she drew her pistol and de Graaf had second thoughts. 'I will not fight a woman', he's reported to have said. So 'in admiration of her courage' he offered her his hand in marriage instead and she accepted. They married in 1693.

A seasoned buccaneer herself, Dieu-le-Veut went to sea with de Graaf and his veteran crew. Dieu-le-Veut and de Graaf had two children, a daughter,

Marie Catherine de Graaf (1694 –1743), and a son – there does not appear to be a record of his name – who died before reaching the age of 5 (1700–1705).

While women aboard a pirate's ship might be considered 'ill-omened' by many, in this instance Dieu-le-Veut's position was welcomed by de Graaf's crew of seasoned veterans. She was seen by his crew as a good luck charm. Unlike Anne Bonny or Mary Read, Dieu-le-Veut did not don men's clothes when sailing with de Graaf and his crew.[13]

De Graaf's unscathed political fluidity among nations failed him. A failure that would cost Dieu-le-Veut and their children three long years in captivity on the Canary Islands as hostages of the English King.

De Graaf spent the summer of 1693 leading buccaneer raids on Jamaica. In May 1695, the English who had previously issued him letters of marque, retaliated against him for an earlier foray against them, by attacking Port-de-Paix (Port of Peace) in Saint Domingue.

English privateer marauders sacked the town and kidnapped de Graaf's family. They were taken by ship and imprisoned in the Canary Islands. The French marine secretary of Pontchartrain heard of their capture, and he wrote to King Louis XIV of France (1638–1715) and asked him to request that the King of Spain intervene. Dieu-le-Veut was not freed until 1698, possibly as a special favour between kings.

Legend has it that Dieu-le-Veut and de Graaf were at sea engaging with the Spanish, when a cannon ball took de Graaf's leg and he died as she took command, soundly beating the Spanish. But there are other reports that de Graaf was sailing again for the French in establishing a colony at the Mississippi near Biloxi when his ship was lost during a hurricane in 1704.

However, Dieu-le-Veut is also reported to have met her maker in modern-day Haiti in 1710, as some say that de Graaf was last spotted off the coast of Louisiana where he was assisting the French in setting up a colony near modern-day Biloxi in Mississippi.

There are conflicting reports about Dieu-le-Veut's final years, and the truth may never be known for certain.

Chapter 4

Neel Cuyper and The Perils of the Great Pox

Pirate:	**Neel Cuyper**
Also known as:	**Neel/Nel/Nell/Nellie Cowper** **Nel/Nell/Nellie Cuyper**
Date of birth:	**1655**
Place of birth:	**Oudewater, Republic of the United Provinces in Holland, Netherlands**
Date of death:	**1695**
Place of death:	**Unknown**

Neel Cuyper, also known to history as Nellie Cowper, was born in Oudewater, Republic of the United Provinces in Holland in the Netherlands during the tempestuous mid-seventeenth century in 1655.

As the Dutch-Portuguese War still raged, Holland had been busy colonising distant lands, including the overseas territories and trading posts controlled and administered by Dutch chartered companies, namely the Dutch East India Company and the Dutch West India Company, which then were chartered by the Crown and later by the Dutch Republic (1581–1795), and afterward by the modern kingdom of the Netherlands until 1815.

We know next to nothing of Cuyper's upbringing or how she found her way to Tortuga Island, other than she was an established crew member aboard a pirate vessel.

> The Buccaneers were robbers, we own, yet they sought something beyond gold. Mansvelt took the Island of St. Catherine and planned a new republic; and Morgan contemplated the destruction of the Bravo Indians. They were outlaws and religious robbers yet genuine and regardful of the minutest delicacies of honour; lovers of freedom, yet obeying the strictest discipline; cruel, yet tender to their friends

> ... All the light and shade of the darkest fiction look poor beside the adventures of these men.[1]

Walter Thornbury reported, in 1861, in his book, *Monarchs of the Main*, many first-person accounts of the men and women who plied Caribbean seas during the Golden Age of Piracy.

A sleek fast sloop of war slid into the harbour at Basse-Terre, the second largest city on Tortuga Island just north of Hispañola. Behind the higgledy-piggledy stretch of motley white-washed and wooden houses stretching along the white sands were vast dark green forests, broad yellow-green, grassy savannahs and mountainous promontories.

Cuyper clutched the ship's gunwales and stared at her new home with some trepidation. For years she had worked tirelessly as a member of the pirate crew and waged war with them, until her gender was accidentally discovered. While some pirate captains like Captain John 'Calico Jack' Rackham had no qualms about having women on board their vessel, others like Captain Ned Low regularly tossed them overboard as unwanted baggage.

Cuyper stared long at the forest's treed with 'cloven' cherry trees, cashew and cacao trees sporting dangling purple pods. The logwood trees were in blossom and fireflies were rising into the night skies from the dark green forests surrounding Basse-Terre. As the sun sank in the Caribbean Sea behind her she watched twinkling night flies lighting the skies along with swarming clouds of mosquitoes.

Piercing the green canopy farther afield were vast pale, green grass savannahs populated with wild cattle and wilder hogs called peccaries. The wild cattle came with explorer Christopher Columbus but were abandoned by their Spanish settlers when threatened by the French and English more than a century later.

Cuyper had been a good and faithful crew'man', but she was being put ashore because she was a woman. Her quartermaster came to her, offering her share of spoils. Her ever-faithful crew reminded her that they were not going to strand her short of cash at Basse-Terre. She had been good to them and they would be good to her.

Other pirate crews might not have been as accommodating, as the articles men signed ofttimes prohibited women from being on board. The infamous

Black Bart's articles stated, 'No woman or young boy is to be allowed on board, and if any man is discovered to be seducing them or taking them to sea in disguise, their punishment is to be death'.[2]

Cuyper had previously served for years aboard Dutch merchantmen, plying the seas between the Canary Islands and the West Indies, until her ship was overtaken by an unknown pirate crew several years before her landing in Basse-Terre. Offered the opportunity to join their pirate crew as an experienced sea hand, she joined them and began her piratical life, preying on the plague of the Caribbean, Spanish shipping.

Tortuga Island is only a small island and it lies in the Antilles an archipelago bordered by the Caribbean Sea to the south and west, the Gulf of Mexico to the north-west, and the Atlantic Ocean to the north and east. Antillean Islands are divided into two smaller groups: the Lesser Antilles and the Greater Antilles. While the Lesser Antilles contains the northerly Leeward Islands, the southeasterly Windward Islands, and the Leeward Antilles just north of Venezuela, the Greater Antilles included the larger islands of Cuba, Jamaica, Puerto Rico, Hispañola and the Cayman Islands.

The Lucayan Archipelago (Turks and Caicos Islands and The Bahamas), though part of the West Indies, are generally not included among the Antillean Islands. Geographically, the Antillean Islands are often considered a subregion of North America.

Tortuga Island was originally settled by native Taíno people. While in the seventeenth century it was frequently home to French, Spanish and English settlers, who warred against each other for control.

We have no idea what Cuyper looked like, although it might be safe to speculate that she was fair-eyed and fair-haired, possibly red-haired, as are many Netherlanders today, but we may never know with certainty what she actually looked like.

It was not all that unusual for women to surreptitiously serve in the Dutch military, especially their navy who employed every 'able-bodied' sea'man' they could lay hands on during their European wars, which spilled into the colonies of the Caribbean.

At the time of Cuyper's arrival at Basse-Terre and Cayona, the two main towns on Tortuga Island were home to diverse populations, the detritus of colonial empires. Basse-Terre was home to the French, English, natives, and men and women who were freed or runaway slaves. Tortuga Island was like a microcosm of Europe, without the Spanish and their indefatigable warships:

> Catholics, Protestants, Puritans, gallants, officers, common-seamen, farmer's sons, men of rank, hunters, sailors, planter's, murderers, fanatics, Creoles, Spaniards, negroes, astrologers, monks, pilots, guides, merchants – all pass before us in a motely, ever-changing *masquerade*.[3]

Basse-Terre was a safe, secure place where pirates of any colour, creed or religion could sell and spend their spoils in pleasure pursuits among a myriad of gambling dens, saloons and brothels, while planning their next 'prize-taking' and taking on stores.

According to Arne Zuidhoek's book *Lady Pirates*,[4] Cuyper adroitly used her spoils to engage in the money trade. As a 'connoisseur of coin' she exchanged 'crowns, pieces-of-eight, doubloons, ducats, piasters and coppers' and lent her spoils money at interest.

Being astute with money gave her an edge over others used to living day to day and she attracted the elites of Basse-Terre, the plantation owners and the captains and quartermasters of successful pirate, privateer or merchant ships.

Zuidhoek reports she was charming and when she was not lending money at interest, she engaged in sex for money with the Basse-Terre elites until an occupational hazard made her ill. Venereal diseases were rife in the Caribbean inns and brothels, and syphilis, the great pox that first plagued French King Charles VIII's (1470–1498) army in 1494 during his assault on Naples, was more virulent than the disease that plagues us still.

For the afflicted, at first genital ulcers appeared and then progressed to a fever, general rash and joint and muscle pains. Months or weeks later the first 'poxes' were followed by large, painful and foul-smelling abscesses and sores or pocks (poxes), all over the body. Muscles and bones became painful, especially at night. Poxes became ulcers that often ate into bones sometimes even destroying the cartilage and soft tissues in the nose, lips and eyes. 'Poxes often extended into the mouth and throat, and ofttimes early death occurred.'

From woodcut drawings at the time and scholarly references, the disease plaguing the Caribbean pirates and privateers was much more severe than syphilis today, with a more rapid mortality. And it was more easily spread, possibly because it was a new version of the disease and the population had no immunity against it.[5]

Author Voltaire wrote later, 'On their flippant way through Italy, the French carelessly picked up Genoa, Naples and syphilis. Then they were thrown out and deprived of Naples and Genoa. But they did not lose everything – syphilis went with them.' By 1497, syphilis had spread across Europe, including Germany, Switzerland, France, Italy, England and Scotland.[6]

At the time, the 'cures' for gonorrhoea and syphilis were often worse than the disease. Gonorrhea, known as 'The Clap', the description arising from the French treatment for the disease, which was to place a man's infected body part inside a book and then to clap it shut, thereby extruding the pus from inside it. Mercury salts and inhalations were used for the great pox, known today as syphilis, with the result that those afflicted often died from mercury poisoning.

While for decades it was believed the Columbus crew brought syphilis to Europe from the Americas, in fact recent archaeological evidence for congenital syphilis was found in the traditional barrel-shaped teeth of two children who died in ancient Egypt thousands of years ago.

Undaunted by her afflictions, and ever resourceful, Cuyper decided to turn lemons into lemonade, and she began a new way of life that would benefit many of her fellows. Moving across the strait to the Island of Hispañola, stretching both east and west of Basse-Terre, on Tortuga Island she settled atop a promontory in a little crescent-shaped bay called La Badi. It is there that Cuyper built her summer home, a chapel and an inn. At the time, Hispañola was a French possession and profits and taxes from its vast sugar cane plantations help build Versailles.

The French buccaneers called the beach below Cuyper's place Cucu Plage, later colloquially shortened to Con-Con Plage, in reference to a woman's genitals 'her cunny' and what could be had from the other women 'boarding' above the sandy beach at Cuyper's place.

Cuyper flourished for a while building an elegant villa overlooking the sea and a chapel to save her soul. As late as 1978 some ruins still remained of her chapel amid ruined walls and crowding creepers.

But Cuyper's paradise was not to last and happily ever after was not to be her fate as her inn was lost along with her life after Spanish and British privateers with a troop of regular soldiers stormed the island razing all they plundered while massacring French settlers, pirates and their hosts during the 1695 invasion of Tortuga Island in the waning days of Nine Years' War between France and the Confederation.

It is certain she was skilled with weapons and even though outnumbered she would surely have fought for her life.

Chapter 5

Jacquotte Delahaye, Real or Phantom?

Pirate:	**Jacquotte Delahaye**
Also known as:	**Back From the Dead Red**
	The Lash
Date of birth:	**1645?**
Place of birth:	**Unknown**
Date of death:	**1678**
Place of death:	**Unknown**

Like many other women in history, controversy surrounds Jacquotte Delahaye. While many arm-chair historians do not believe Delahaye existed, others maintain there are glimpses of history in the stories told about her. Like so many other women in history whether she actually lived or not is open to speculation. While some attribute her existence to the novel written by French journalist Leon Treich in the 1940s, others remain unconvinced.

If we accept, she did, indeed, live as have so many other anonymous women left out of the pages of history written by men, this might be her story.

Supposedly, Delahaye was born in Haiti to a French father and a Haitian mother. She survived a brutal childhood. Her mother died while giving birth to her younger brother, who was brain damaged at birth. Delahaye raised and cared for him. A few years later, her father was killed in a knife fight during a card game, leaving Delahaye with little money to look after herself and her brother. Other would-be historians claim her father was killed during a Spanish raid on Saint Domingue aided by British Royal Navy personnel[1], possibly confusing her fate with that of Neel Cuyper.

Purportedly, renowned as a red-haired beauty, she was forced into sex work and then to piracy in order to care for her brother.

At the beginning of the Golden Age of Piracy, Delahaye would have been about 20 years old. She reportedly worked as a barmaid, as a lady's maid and in a brothel before beginning her pirating pursuits. Unlike other female pirates, Delahaye's pirating profession, apparently, did not depend on her relationships with male pirates.[2]

As a pirate, she was reportedly ruthless and successful in skirmishing at sca. Much given to violent excesses and harsh discipline, she earned the moniker, 'The Lash'.[3]

She is believed by some (although no actual contemporary reports survive of her accomplishments and travails) to have captured Fort de la Rocher on Tortuga Island, wresting it from Spanish hands when she was only 26 years old (in 1671).[4] It is implausible she did this alone. Some claim she was afterward appointed advisor to the governor of Tortuga Island, but there is no documentary evidence.

In 1670, the English buccaneer Henry Morgan hid his piratical activities under the legal veneer of French letters of marque, and as a privateer he actively promoted Tortuga Island as a base of operations and for the disposal of plundered booty.

Five-hundred buccaneers from Tortuga Island and a thousand buccaneers from Jamaica, under the command of Morgan set sail in 1670. They attacked and plundered Santa Marta in Columbia, Rio de la Hacha (sometimes referred to as Riohacha) also in Columbia, Puerto Bello in Puerto Rico and Panama. Morgan was thanked by the Council of Jamaica in May 1671 for his privateer activities. In the same year, he sailed to England and in 1672 was incarcerated in the Tower of London solely to placate the Spanish ambassador (for appearances sake). Morgan was treated as a hero on his arrival in London.[5]

By 1670, many Caribbean buccaneers went legally pirating under letters of marque for the governor of Tortuga Island. They also settled on the coast of Saint Domingue. Others wandered off to other colonies in the Caribbean. Despite the attempts of governor Bertrand d'Ogeron de La Bouëre these settlers continued to trade with the Dutch. They obtained African slaves and most of their stores from them in exchange for tobacco and ginger. Tortuga Island's elites had vast plantations of tobacco growing inland.[6]

Around Tortuga Island the governor eventually managed to control the trading activities of the buccaneers somewhat by employing a regular squadron of frigates that drove the Dutch traders away. The buccaneers from Tortuga Island and Saint Domingue were used as a strike force and a means to supplement French forces in their attempts to gain a larger foothold in the Caribbean.[7] It is not impossible, if Delahaye existed, that she sailed among them.

When the lieutenant general of the French Antilles, Jean Charles Baas, attacked Curaçao in March 1673 he was expecting help from Tortuga Island. But the assistance from Tortuga Island failed to materialise, as the fleet was shipwrecked on the coast of Puerto Rico, where the crews fell into Spanish hands and were treated as pirates. (They were executed.)[8]

Some historians claim that Delahaye plied the seas with Marie-Anne Dieu-le-Veut, but I have found no documentary evidence that the two women knew each other. That is not to say if Delahaye did exist, that they were not acquainted, as women were sometimes scarce in the Caribbean.

Others claim Delahaye was cornered during a skirmish, and to escape her pursuers she faked her own death and took on a *nom de guerre*, a male alias, and lived as a man for many years. Upon her return to Tortuga Island, she became known as 'Back From the Dead Red' because of her striking red hair.[9]

It is believed that Delahaye died defending Tortuga Island.[10]

Chapter 6

Gráinne O'Malley, Pirate Queen of Connacht

Pirate:	Gráinne O'Malley
Also known as:	Bald Grace
	Dark Lady of Doona
	Granny Imallye
	Grace/Gráinne O'Flaherty
	Grace/Gráinne Ó Fhlaithbertaigh/
	Ó Flatharthaigh/Ó Flaithbertaigh/
	Ó Flaithbheartaigh
	Grace of the Gamblers
	Grace O'Malley
	Gráinne/Grace O'Mallie
	Grany O'Maly
	Gráinne Mhaol
	Gráinne/Grace Uí Máille
Date of birth:	1530
Place of birth:	Umhaill, Ireland
Married:	Richard-na-Iarainn Burke
	Dónal 'of the Battle' Ó Flatharthaigh
	(also known as Dónal Ó Fhlaithbertaigh and
	Dónal Ó Flaithbheartaigh)
Date of death:	1603
Place of death:	Rockfleet Castle, Ireland

'The Irish were never tamed with words but with swords',[1] complained Sir Richard Bingham, appointed provisional president of Connaught (in Ireland) by English Queen Elizabeth I (Elizabeth Tudor) (1533–1603) in 1584. And he was right.

Rotting corpses inside cast-iron 'crow's cages' adorned the Wapping Street stairs along the River Thames, a warning to all would-be pirates that the only pirating Elizabeth I would allow was that which gave her advantage. Gráinne O'Malley, Ireland's aging notorious pirate queen must have sighed as she sailed past them. She had just escaped a threatened hanging.

In her hands she held a letter of introduction to Elizabeth I's spymaster and chief privy councillor Lord Burghley, written by a business acquaintance, Black Tom Butler, 10th Earl of Ormond, who was Elizabeth I's relative. Burghley was curious about the woman who 'over-stepped the role of womanhood.'[2] He sent her a letter, a questionnaire of eighteen questions regarding her life, her crimes, her family and her religion.

But Burghley kept her from meeting the English queen until late summer, when O'Malley sailed to Greenwich to met her. At 63, O'Malley was a seasoned military commander both on land and sea, who had personally led her troops into battle and who had survived two husbands and her eldest son's untimely death during more than forty years of internecine Irish warfare between the clans and the occupying forces of the British Crown.

Elizabeth I, the 'Virgin Queen', came face to face with pirate queen O'Malley, whom some sources claim had hidden a dagger for the English monarch inside her boot, should their conversation go sideways.

Both queens were extraordinary women who challenged the patriarchal societies of their times. But there were major differences between them. O'Malley at 63 had borne three sons and a daughter, buried two husbands and one son, and had her lands, cattle and horses seized by the British Crown. Her youngest son, Theobald 'Tibbot na Long' ('Tibbot of the Ships'), was facing a horrifically painful traitor's death and was languishing imprisoned in Dublin Castle, begin held by Elizabeth I's governor, Sir Richard Bingham. Being drawn (eviscerated) and quartered while being repeatedly hanged by the neck was the execution of choice by the British Crown for treason.

Just before she sailed for England, O'Malley had narrowly escaped hanging herself. By contrast Elizabeth I had bravely survived her father's reign, palace intrigues and her sister's religious pogroms before Queen Mary I (Mary Tudor) (1516–1558) died.

Multiple assassination attempts against Elizabeth I coloured who she favoured. In 1593, she was continuing apace the colonisation of Ireland, as had her father King Henry VIII (1491–1547). Considered a weak link in her reign, Ireland was a duplicitous, 'warring island filled with Catholics and savages', according to some at the time.

At 60, Elizabeth I was at the zenith of her power, while O'Malley had come seeking solace and favour, and the life of her youngest son. But O'Malley did not bow to Elizabeth I, saying that 'one queen should not bow to another'. Both women spoke to each other in Latin, the language of God at the time, although it is obvious in her later letters to Elizabeth I that O'Malley was fluent in English, too.

An aging Elizabeth I was sumptuously dressed and wore a bright red wig to cover her greying, spartan hair. Her face was carefully painted with rice powder and blushed with rose, and framed by a magnificent, white Tudor ruff. As was her usual attire, she was bedecked with pearls.

Described as 'stout', O'Malley was an on the run refugee from the predations of Elizabeth I's appointed governor, but she was eloquent in her pleadings. As a mother, she fiercely begged for the life of her youngest son, whose capture she viewed as no more than an act – less of his 'opposition to the Crown' – but as a strategy by the governor of Connacht designed to bring O'Malley and her soldiers, sailors and pirates to heel. Correspondence emanating from this meeting confirmed, as O'Malley attested, 'the clemencie and favour'[3] she received from the queen.

Legend has it that Elizabeth I offered O'Malley the title of Countess of Connacht, but she reportedly refused. Elizabeth I immediately ordered the release of O'Malley's son and restored him to his lands. She also gave her royal assent so that O'Malley could return to her lands and continue her work, which was described as 'maintenance by land and sea' without hindrance.

When Elizabeth I subsequently ordered a new map drawn of Ireland, 'Grany O'Maly' was the only woman listed as helming clan lands. This meeting between two women, one who loved her pirates and one who was a renowned pirate queen, resulted in the anglicisation of the O'Malleys for generations. But life had never been easy for O'Malley.

Little more than half a century earlier, Eoghan – Owen in English – Dubhdara Uí Máille of Umhall (a Gaelic territory in what is now Clew Bay in western County Mayo, Ireland) and his wife, Margaret, daughter of Conchobhar O'Malley, were blessed with the birth of a daughter. Eoghan named her Gráinne – Grace in English. Like many other pirate women, O'Malley was to have many names with varied spellings.

Living in Iar Connacht (modern-day Connemara) in Ireland, the Uí Máilles and their neighbours the O'Flahertys were strong, independent, wealthy sea-faring clans, originally part of the Kingdom of Connaught, who paid tribute to their 'betters' and extracted tribute from others.

The Uí Máilles had been landed Irish aristocracy since the thirteenth century. Their family motto was '*Terra Marique Potens*' ('Powerful on Land and Sea').[4] Eoghan, like his father before him, although hot headed, was an enterprising young man who earned a good living from the sea and the land. Avoiding English patrols, he clandestinely ferried Scottish mercenaries, and he collected tolls from all shipping passing through Uí Máille controlled waters and when opportunity presents itself, he engaged in a bit of piracy. Frequently, he traded raw resources like wool and ale for luxury items. He traded internationally with the Scots as well as with France, Libya and Spain.

At the time of O'Malley's birth, Henry VIII sat on the throne of England and was embroiled in a political, religious and domestic reformation with a messy, non-papally sanctioned divorce of his first wife. He succeeded in divorcing Spain's Catholic Catherine of Aragon with whom he had been wed for twenty years and married Reformist Anne Boleyn, and in 1533 Boleyn gave birth to Elizabeth, the future queen of England.

In 1542 to the dismay of many, Henry VIII claimed the title and was declared King of Ireland by the Irish Parliament. At the time, Ireland was a nation divided. Most of the coastal cities, and Dublin and its surrounding counties were occupied by the landed, occupying English who regarded the Irish hinterland filled with vicious, warring clans, with trepidation and foreboding. For the English, Dublin was like ancient Rome, in that it was surrounded by uncivilised, blood-thirsty barbarians. The country outside English control was populated by the native Irish and the Gaelicised Old English or descendants of Normans.

Outside the English sphere of influence, living within independent territories the Irish clans thrived on traditional and non-taxable pursuits like poaching castles, stealing cattle and opportunistic piracy. All the while vying for clan domination through blood feuding and inter-marriage.

Like today's Mafia, a rigid system of clan clientship existed; with weaker families aligning with more powerful ones. Bonds of loyalty were forged by means of tribute, military aid, fosterage and inter-marriage. This complex interdependency bound Irish families in a hierarchical society in which loyalty, status and honour were all important. The Uí Máilles were clients of MacWilliam (clan leader) Íachtarach of the Mayo Bourkes, and in turn, they had weaker clan clients of their own. Gaelic law on lineage legitimised a clan leader's power over other clans in a rigid hierarchical system.

After Henry VIII's declaration as King of Ireland, he and future English monarchs would no longer be content with the Irish *status quo*, or the isolated status of the occupying English. A series of legal measures were introduced into Ireland by Henry VIII establishing a centralised system of government, and attempts were made to acculturate and Anglicise the entire population, including through the introduction of widespread education through parish schools.

When O'Malley was 7 years old, as part of a burgeoning humanistic movement for social and cultural reform, an act for 'the English order, habit and language'[5] was passed in the Dublin Parliament in 1537, which established primary schools in every parish for the teaching of the English language and culture and religion. It also forbade the use of Gaelic, even in the Irish Parliament.

Prior to this Act, education operated though a series of bardic schools, which ensured the hereditary nature of traditional leaning. It is likely O'Malley, as a daughter of the landed aristocracy, would have accessed this diverse, bardic education taught by the Irish *literati*. But it is also reported that at the age of 8, she accompanied her father aboard his ships while raiding.

Many in Ireland decried Henry VIII's attempts to 'civilise' and acculturate the Irish, Eoghan O'Malley was among them. However, other Irish nobles opted for client clan status, rather than war and fighting the English Crown.

Henry VIII's offer of 'surrender and regrant' proved attractive to many of Ireland's ruling élite, and in 1541 the MacWilliam Uachtarach of the Galway Bourkes became the Earl of Clanricard. In 1542, Hugh O'Neill capitulated and was made Earl of Tyrone. While Gerald FitzJames FitzGerald (sometimes referred to as Gerald FitzJames) was declared 15th Earl of Desmond and

Murrough O'Brien was named Earl of Thomand. Neither the MacWilliam Íachtarach nor the Uí Máille took the king's offer.

During the Tudor conquest of Ireland (*c.*1540–1603), 'surrender and regrant' was the legal mechanism by which traditional Irish clans were disempowered from their traditional power structure rooted in kinship and clan, in exchange for the mantle of a late feudal-fealty system governed by English law. This change would profoundly impact O'Malley's future.

Henry VIII wanted the Irish to adopt English rule. Under English law, women were treated very differently from the way they lived under Irish Brehon law, which provided numerous freedoms to women that were not granted under English law. The Irish marriage law, known as the Couple's Law, allowed ten different types of unions, each with its own responsibilities and rules. Among the most egalitarian of these was the union of mutual contribution, wherein the wife and her husband brought an equal amount of property to the marriage. Mutual consent was required for some contracts, while either party could create others. The law also codified seduction and rape, both of which were defined as crimes, and there were penalties for these crimes.

According to gender, Irish law allowed for fourteen reasons for divorce. A man could divorce his wife if she were unfaithful, while a woman could divorce her husband if he abused her. Under English law, only one type of union was allowed, though two forms of marriage, contract and canonical, existed.

Under English law, like in ancient Roman, husbands were the head of his household, with all owing obedience to him. Divorce was not permitted, though a legal separation could be granted by the Church if enough proof was gathered, and the separation was based upon legal grounds. After the English conquest of Ireland and imposition of English common law, Irish married women lost their marriage rights and effectively became second-class citizens.[6]

'Surrender and regrant' was an official attempt to incorporate the clan chiefs into the English-controlled Kingdom of Ireland, and to guarantee clan property under English common law, as opposed to the traditional Irish Brehon law system. This strategy was the primary non-violent method Crown officials in Dublin Castle used to subjugate Irish clan leaders and to saddle their heirs with obeisance to the English Crown.

O'Malley was 8 when she accompanied her father on one of his trading/raiding vessels and she fell in love with the sea. But her mother wanted her properly educated as was required of the Irish aristocracy and she was supposed to learn Spanish, French and Latin. We know now that her mother succeeded at least with Latin, which she spoke with Elizabeth I when they met years later.

O'Malley loved the freedom she enjoyed being at sea with her father and some historians allege she was actually aloft in the rigging when their ship was boarded by the English, who briefly held her father hostage. O'Malley was reported to have dropped from the rigging onto one of his assailants, allowing him and his crew to regain control of their ship.

During her teen years, O'Malley begged her mother to allow her to go trading with her father to Spain. After being told her long red hair would be caught in the rigging, she reportedly cut it off, dressed as a boy, earning her the moniker of 'Gráinne Mhaol' or 'Bald Grace'. While still a teen, she developed a taste for cards and gambling, and she was so accomplished that she was sometimes known as Grace of the Gamblers.

O'Malley travelled with her father on his trading trips and by the age of 16, she was a fiercely loyal and a seasoned hand at sea, when her father married her to Dónal 'of the Battle' Ó Flatharthaigh (sometimes spelt Ó Fhlaithbertaigh, Ó Flaithbertaigh and Ó Flaithbheartaigh, and Dónal sometimes used the surname O'Flaherty).

Ó Flatharthaigh was the *Tánaiste* of the Flatharthaigh clan, and a good match for O'Malley, as the daughter of the chief of the Uí Máille clan. Ambitiously, Ó Flatharthaigh hoped to one day become the lord of Iar Connacht, roughly Connemara today.

During their twenty-year marriage she bore him two sons, Eóghain Ó Flatharthaigh and Murchad (sometimes spelt Murchadh) Ó Flatharthaigh, and a daughter, Meaḋḃ Ní (meaning daughter of – the equivalent of Ó in the male name) Flatharthaigh. (The children sometimes used the surname O'Flaherty.)

But Dónal Ó Flatharthaigh ambitions to become Lord of Connacht were thwarted when Elizabeth I chose his kinsman, Murrough (sometimes spelt Murchad or Murchadh) na dTuadh 'of the Battleaxes' Ó Flatharthaigh (sometimes referred to as na dTuadh O'Flaherty) to be the Lord of Connacht, so his assume the title Sir Murrough.

In 1565, Dónal Ó Flatharthaigh was killed during an ambush while hunting in the hills surrounding Lough Comb. Undoubtedly, his assassination was part of Ó Flatharthaigh and O'Malley's long-standing struggle against Clan Joyce for control of Hen's Castle on Lough Corrib in County Galway. When the Joyces stormed their castle, thinking O'Malley would not resist, she held her ground, fought back successfully and forced Clan Joyce into a routed retreat.

Leaving her children to maintain a continued defence of Ó Flatharthaigh's patrimony, and taking a thousand soldiers with her, O'Malley returned to her ancestral lands in Clew Bay setting up house in the castle on the Island of Clare now called Caisleán Ghráinne in Irish.

Some historians allege that while there, she took a shipwrecked sailor as a lover, but her affair was brief as he was murdered by members of Clan MacMahon of Ballyvoy (in Ireland – modern-day Northern Ireland). Claiming blood justice for him O'Malley attacked Clan MacMahon's stronghold at Doona Castle in Blacksod Bay. She faced his killers on Caher Island and killed them in retribution. This act of blood justice earned her the moniker of 'Dark Lady of Doona'.[7]

O'Malley took another husband, Richard-na-Iarainn, in 1566, with whom she had a son, Theobald.

Richard-na-Iarainn Bourke (sometimes spelt Burke) was a master mariner and the two of them became the plague of the western seas of Ireland, using their fleet of swift, sure galleys to terrorise and exhort 'black rent' from ships plying coastal shipping lanes. Black rent was a levy for passing though clan-controlled waters.

Elizabeth I's Lord Deputy of Ireland Sir Henry Sidney (1529–1586) wrote in his memoirs, 'She was as well by sea as by land and more than a master's mate for him.'[8]

O'Malley's maritime pillaging activities attracted the attention of the English government, which led to an unsuccessful siege of her castle at Rockfleet in March 1574. Undeterred by words alone, afterward she sailed to Dublin, putting in at Howth where she kidnapped the son of the lord of Howth, whom she held for ransom.[9]

During Sidney's third term in office, his task was to introduce a new taxation system known as 'composition'. Having met with little success, he returned in 1576 and summoned the lords to a meeting, during which he met 'a most feminine sea captain called Granny Imallye who offered her services onto me'. Although he did not avail of her 'three galleys and two hundred fighting men', he did sail with her to inspect the seaward defences of Galway, a service for which she successfully billed him. Sidney noted her show of strength and concluded that 'This was a notorious woman in all the coasts of Ireland'.

Within weeks of her offer to Sidney, O'Malley set off to plunder Desmond; she was captured off Thormond by Gerald Fitz James Fitzpatrick, 15th Earl of Desmond and held in Limerick Gaol to be used as a bargaining chip. During her captivity Lord Grey de Wilton succeeded Sidney. The MacWilliam was forced to submit to the Crown, and Richard-na-Iarainn Bourke's future as successor was no longer a foregone conclusion.

In 1578, Desmond handed O'Malley over to Lord Justice Drury. This 'demonstration of his loyalty ... sending unto you Grany O'Mayle' impressed Elizabeth I's Privy Council. O'Malley was transferred to Dublin Castle in chains. She was later released in 1579 after 'her promise to mend her ways' and by March 1579 was ensconced in Carraigahowley (Rockfleet Castle), where she was then besieged by Captain Martin, sent with orders to capture her for attacks on Galway shipping. Martin was lucky to evade capture himself, 'so spirited was the defence made by the extraordinary woman', he wrote.

During her captivity, her husband had not been idle, having become embroiled in a Catholic rebellion hosted by the FitzGeralds/FitzJameses. Not liking the architects of the plan, O'Malley did everything she could to rehabilitate Bourke's nebulous standing with the Crown. After successful negotiations, in 1580, Bourke regained his right to the tile of MacWilliam. In October 1582, at the height of their powers at sea and on land, the couple sparkled at a gathering of the Connacht nobility. While at the residence of the provincial governor Sir Nicholas Malby, one observer noticing her confidence among all commented, 'Grace O'Maly thinketh herself to be no small lady'.[10]

A consummate politician and negotiator, when necessary, in January 1583, when tax collector Theobald Dillon's soldiery encamped on her land demanding arears of £600 in unpaid taxes, she was gracious and entertaining, plying him and his men with wine and food, while she inveigled the cancellation of her debts to the English Crown. She also gave Malby 300 head of cattle.

Fortunes are made, won and lost. Her fortunes shifted in 1584 after Malby died on 3 March, and the governorship passed to Sir Richard Bingham – a stern taskmaster – not easily bribed with words or cattle. She and Bingham were at odds and then and even more so after her husband abruptly died in September 1584.

Acting for members of his family, she aided their escape from Bingham's mercenary troops when he laid siege to the Bourke's Lough Mask Castle. The following June, O'Malley was arrested by Captain John Bingham, the governor's brother, for her role in the Connacht rebellion. He treated her brutally and bound her in ropes and chains, taking her to Henry Sidney's encampment, where he threatened to hang her. Her stepson Richard Bourke (junior) interceded, pledging his own son as hostage in her place.

Fate turned its back to O'Malley, when in July 1585 her eldest son by Ó Flatharthaigh, Murchad Ó Flatharthaigh, was lured and then cruelly murdered by Bingham's mercenaries. Then the Bourkes' brutal revolt against the Crown sent her fleeing for sanctuary. She took her galleys and her men to Ulster and hid her ships and crews among the O'Neills and O'Donnells until peace was restored. To keep the peace, she pledged her youngest son, Theobald, as hostage to Bingham while she sailed to Dublin to receive the queen's pardon on 4 May 1588.[11]

But peace in Ireland has always been elusive and during the cold winter of February 1589, Richard Bourke killed John Browne the Sheriff of Mayo. He led an uprising of Catholic nobility from County Mayo and northern Galway. In retribution, County Mayo was devasted by regular English troops under Bingham's command. O'Malley supported the rebellion by ferrying Scots mercenaries to the fray to fight on side with the Bourkes.

A year later, the rebellion failed, while Bourke won favourable terms for himself, O'Malley fought on attacking the Isle of Arran and devastating the towns and villages there before asking for quarter under Bourke's surety and protection.

In June 1591, O'Malley was fighting Scots raiders, but she was harassed at sea by Bingham's galleys. His navy began dominating her waters, undermining her ability to control shipping along the western coast and earn a living. At the same time, Bingham arrested her youngest son, Theobald, on charges of treason, as well as her only blood brother Domhnall an Piopa O'Malley of Westport. With Sir Murrough na dTuadh Ó Flatharthaigh she sailed to London to petition the queen to save her son.

When she finally reached Elizabeth I's ear, she found common ground with the English monarch who immediately ordered an investigation into Bingham's egregious governorship. O'Malley returned to Ireland in September and by early December both her son and brother were freed.

But her conflicts with Bingham only increased and in 1594 he quartered his troops on her lands. Once again, enlisting the help of Elizabeth I's cousin Black Thomas Butler, 10th Earl of Ormond, who championed her cause in a letter to the Privy Council on 19 April 1595. As her seaborne fortunes waned, O'Malley tried to obtain her share of her late husband's estate, but she was thwarted by her son Murchad Ó Flatharthaigh who had no intention of losing a third of his lands to her.

Traitorously, her son preferred life under the English common law, which gave him a greater share of the estate than he would have had under Irish Brehon law. Returning to raiding and extorting 'black rent' in trying once again to make a living from the sea, in 1596, O'Malley went north raiding Thomond and the Scottish lands of MacNeill of Barna.

Finally worn out during the Nine Years' War, O'Malley sided with the English Crown persuading her sons to do likewise. In August 1597, all three of them earned a fee of £200 (British currency) for their service to the Crown, but a year later they were punished when the forces of Hugh O'Neill and Red Hugh O'Donnell who had previously been her allies and given her sanctuary invaded Connacht and devastated her lands.[12]

Undaunted and unbowed, O'Malley was still breathing and raiding in July 1601. Historians believe she died in the same year as Elizabeth I in 1603. She was interred on the Island of Clare off the coast of County Mayo having outlived two husbands, one son, and having outwitted many, many of the men who opposed her and her family on land and sea.

Chapter 7

Sayyida al-Hurra, Queen of the Barbary Pirates

Pirate:	Sayyida al-Hurra
Birth name:	Sayyida al-Hurra ibn Banu Rashid al-Mandri el-Outassi Hakima Tatwan (possibly Aisha)
Also known as:	The Islamic Pirate
Date of birth:	1485 (or 890 *Hijri*)
Place of birth:	Unknown
Married:	Ahmed el-Outassi (also known as Abu al-Abbas Ahmed ibn Muhammad or Sultan Ahmed) Sultan of Morocco Abou Hassan al-Mandri, Sultan of Tétouan
Date of death:	1561
Place of death:	Unknown

Storm clouds menacingly boiled across the horizon as Sayyida al-Hurra scanned the choppy Mediterranean Sea whipping white caps in the Strait of Gibraltar, connecting the Atlantic Ocean to the Mediterranean Sea. She and her twenty-man crew were helming a tartane, a 45-foot-long wooden vessel with dual masts and lateen sails, much like any other Mediterranean fisherman or merchant's swift coastal vessel.

Although her ship may have looked like any other innocuous trading vessel, al-Hurra's swift corsair concealed beneath canvas shrouds four cast iron cannon, wooden boxes filled with muskets and ten swivel guns. Al-Hurra was not out for trade, she was engaged in the world's second oldest profession, and it was not soldiering, it was piracy.

At the time, much of the western coastline of North Africa from modern-day Libya to Morocco, was known as the 'Barbary Coast' – a name purloined from a conglomerate of tribal peoples collectively and colonially known as Berbers to those who lived there.

Barbary Coast pirates were a major threat to Mediterranean marine commerce for more than 200 years, and they preferred the swift, small, easily manoeuvrable tartane as most European ships captains were lulled into a false sense of security, as they did not recognise them as threatening pirate vessels from afar.

Barbary Coast pirates existed long before and after Caribbean pirates plied their perilous Atlantic and Gulf coast seas. These pirates like al-Hurra robbed ships on the high seas and captured slaves and villagers in raids along the Mediterranean and Atlantic coasts. The slave markets of Marrakesh and Algiers teamed with Europeans captured and sold or held for ransom – sometimes for years – by pirates. Those who were not ransomed by family and friends faced a lifetime of frequently brutal slavery.

But al-Hurra was not sailing, robbing and raiding for booty. She plied the high seas for blood justice and revenge, and during this raid she had secured in the hold of her vessel the kidnapped and terrified wife of the Portuguese governor. Al-Hurra was certain the governor's wife would bring a fine ransom and cause him and the other colonial powers to think twice when they sailed Barbary Coast waters. Her nimble crew begged Allah to deliver them from the savage storm that swept them threatening all their lives and the others sailing with her.

One ship would never make port and despite the captain's valiant efforts, al-Hurra grimly watched as one tartane took on water, then suddenly capsized, sending its crew to their makers, and the ship, laden with goods and slaves from Europe, to the bottom, to rest among the ghosts of other ancient mariners who had failed to overcome unpredictable storms while navigating the Strait of Gibraltar.

'Less famous than the pirates of the Caribbean, the corsair capital of Algiers turned to piracy far earlier and was a much bigger business…', said Sean Kingsley, editor-in-chief of *Wreckwatch* magazine,[1] during an interview about a 2007 tartane discovery in the Strait of Gibraltar.

Sayyida al-Hurra ibn Banu Rashid al-Mandri el-Outassi Hakima Tatwan is a long name for a remarkable Muslim woman. Translated, Sayyida al-Hurra is an honorific meaning a daughter or descendant of Muhammed, 'noble lady who is free and independent; the woman sovereign who bows to no superior authority.' Hakima Tatwan translates as 'wise ruler of Tétouan'.[2]

Believed to have been born in the Moorish kingdom of Granada in southern Spain around 1485, al-Hurra was the daughter of Lalla Zohra Fernandez, from Vejer de la Frontera, a Christian convert to Islam, and Moulay Ali ibn Rashid, who was from a prominent aristocratic Muslim family. Al-Hurra's birth name may have been Aisha.[3] She had an older brother, Moulay Ibrahim ibn Rashid. The family lived in the Andalusian kingdom of Granada, although not for long.

The Emirate of Granada was the last Nasrid dynasty-ruled area in the Iberian Peninsula of Spain. In January 1492, after ten years of civil war, Sultan Muhammad XII (known in Europe as Boabdil) of Granada surrendered the Moorish Emirate to Catholic forces led by King Ferdinand II of Aragon and Queen Isabella I of Castile, who took over the sultan's royal palace, the Alhambra, then described by poets as a 'pearl amid emeralds', words carved in Arabic along the Alhambra's stone walls, still visible today.

Signed in November 1491, the Treaty of Granada guaranteed Muslim rights, including religious tolerance and fair treatment, in return for the capitulation. However, the guarantees did not last and forced conversions to Christianity, expropriation of personal property, imprisonments and executions, led to 100 years of uprisings by the 250,000 Moors residing in southern Spain. Muslims had settled in southern Spain for 800 years.

A few months after signing the treaty and with money from Moorish expropriations, Isabella I agreed to fund Christopher Columbus's explorations to find a western sea route to China, India, and the fabled spice islands of Asia. Columbus sailed for the New World with three ships in August of 1492.

Al-Hurra's family was from the Nasrid aristocracy and were forced to flee their homes during the bloody fighting, and pogroms by Christian Spain prior to the 1491 treaty. Al-Hurra and the surviving members of her family fled as refugees to Chefchaouen in Morocco on the North African continent.

The Rashids were an aristocratic family, who claimed descent from the Prophet Muhammad through Idrisi I, founder in the eighth century of Morocco's first Islamic dynasty. Soon after the family's exile from Granada, they settled in the Rif Mountains south-east of Tangier, where Moulay Ali ibn Rashid founded the city-state of Chefchaouen, near Morocco's northern coast. Recognising the need for sanctuary, Rashid opened Chefchaouen's gates to waves of Andalusian refugees fleeing the Spanish Reconquista – the centuries long effort to reclaim Spanish Muslim lands for Christendom.

While al-Hurra's childhood was reported to have been happy and secure, her happiness was constantly over shadowed by the trauma her family suffered during the civil war and their forced exile from the wealth and luxury in Granada. As a teen, she would dedicate her life to avenging their exile.

In 1501, at the age of 16, al-Hurra was married to a man thirty years her senior, a friend of her father's, Abou Hassan al-Mandri, Sultan of Tétouan. As was common in aristocratic families at the time, she had been promised to the sultan when she was a small child.[4] (Some scholars believe she married his son instead.)

At the time, al-Mandri had been governor of Tétouan for five years, a small, slightly inland coastal city nestled at the base of the Rif Mountains hugging the Mediterranean coast. Tétouan had been utterly destroyed by the Spanish in 1400 and was still being rebuilt piecemeal by Andalusian exiles like al-Hurra's family in the 1490s.

Tétouan grew on the steep slopes of the Jebel Dersa mountains. One of Morocco's only two ports, Tétouan faced the island of Gibraltar and the sparkling blue Mediterranean Sea. Despite her aristocratic lineage, salt seas ran in al-Hurra's blood. As a noblewoman, she received an education denied most common women. Al-Hurra was multilingual, speaking Portuguese and Castilian Spanish, among other tongues. One of her teachers was famed Moroccan scholar Abdallah al-Ghazwani, whose father, the most erudite Shaykh Oudjal, supposedly once put his hand to al-Hurra's head and declared, 'This girl will rise high in rank.'[5]

Al-Hurra and al-Mandri used their resources to rebuild Tétouan, first building an impressive security wall with seven embedded gates around the city, which remain to this day. According to sixteenth-century historian Al Hasan ibn Muhammad al-Wazzan (later known as Leo Africanus), who wrote a century later about the city's founding father, 'He [al-Mandri] rebuilt the city walls, erected a fort and … waged many a war with the Portuguese, often attacking Ceuta, Ksar and Tangier.'[6]

Al-Mandri was so impressed with al-Hurra's keen insight, intelligence and her judgment that he made her Tétouan's prefect. It was as prefect that al-Hurra first became interested in preying on Portuguese and Spanish ships, looting their wealth and enslaving prisoners in order to fund her vengeance, and as a ready supply of silver and gold for the further restoration of the city.

At the same time as she became prefect, her brother Moulay Ibrahim ibn Rashid was appointed *vizier* to Ahmed al-Wattasi, Sultan of Fez. Thereby the Rashid family positioned themselves as power players in efforts to unify Morocco against the rising colonial European powers of Portugal and Spain.

During their marriage, she became allied with infamous Turkish corsair Oruç Kemal Reis (1474–1518), the noted Barbary Coast pirate (known to Europeans as Barbarossa of Algiers). Al-Mandri died nine years after their marriage, and in 1515 al-Hurra assumed the legitimate governorship of Tétouan, by then a growing trading, and raiding centre teeming with Moroccan pirates.

Now, firmly allied with Reis, al-Hurra's ships preyed on Portuguese and Spanish shipping, and her fleet of swift corsairs controlled the western Mediterranean Sea, while Reis wreaked havoc in the eastern Mediterranean.

Born on the island of Lesbos around 1474, Reis and his older brother, Hayreddin, were infamous Barbary Coast corsairs. Much like future privateers, licensed to piracy by their governments, Reis and his brother moved among Mediterranean ports as trusted sailors and servants of the Ottoman sultan. They raided French, Spanish, Portuguese and Italian enclaves and ships, fighting battles against the Knights Hospitallers, and in 1504 they even dared an attack on the much larger flagship of Pope Julius II.

Feared by Europeans for his ferocity, Reis having lost an arm in battle, sported a silver prosthetic arm. Despite his disability, according to eyewitnesses, he: 'fought to the very last gasp, like a lion.'[7] Despite his fearsome ferocity, for six years between 1504 and 1510, dodging Spanish warship patrols, he ferried Muslim/Andalusian refugees from imminent persecution and death in Spain to sanctuary in North Africa. This earned him the appellation of Baba Oruç (also known as Father Oruç). Europeans garbled his spoken name as 'Barbarossa', which translates as 'Redbeard' in Italian. The Germans called him Kaiser RotBart – Caesar Redbeard. However, his beard colour remains a mystery.

While seizing Christian ships buoyed al-Hurra's dreams of vengeance, piracy became an addictive pursuit and was tantalisingly profitable, especially for the merchants in Tétouan. Al-Hurra became one of the wealthiest women in Morocco.

In 1520, her ships captured the wife of the governor of Portugal, whom she held for ransom, months later bartering for the luckless woman's release with the Portuguese government.

Although she had attained more wealth than she had ever imagined, her anger toward the Christians, who had murdered family and friends, and forced her family to flee from their homes in Granada, became a vengeful obsession.

As governor of Tétouan, she met and married the Sultan of Morocco, Ahmed el-Outassi (also known as Abu al-Abbas Ahmed ibn Muhammad or Sultan Ahmed), who ruled from 1526 to 1549 as the sultan of the Moroccan Wattasid dynasty.

However, al-Hurra refused to be married in el-Outassi's capital, Fez, and for the only time in Moroccan history, the ruling sultan married outside the capital in Tétouan. Contemporaries believed al-Hurra insisted on this display of will, to demonstrate to everyone that she was not going to give up governing Tétouan. Even though she married the sultan, she would retain her independence, and she did not become a part of his cloistered hareem. She would rule from the courts of Tétouan and Fez. Some scholars believe al-Hurra was the last person in Islamic history to legitimately hold the title of 'al-Hurra', meaning queen.

The Wattasids were a Zanata Berber ruling dynasty in Morocco, like the Marinids. Although the two families were related, and the Marinids recruited many *viziers* from the Wattasids, these *viziers* assumed the powers of the sultans, seizing power when the last Marinid sultan, Abu Muhammad Abd al-Haqq, who had massacred many of the Wattasids in 1459, was murdered during a popular revolt in Fez in 1465.

Abu Abd Allah al-Sheikh Muhammad ibn Yahiya al-Mahdi became the first Wattasid sultan and was el-Outassi's grandfather.

The Wattasids controlled only the northern part of Morocco, while southern Morocco was divided into several, often warring, principalities. El-Outassi was the sultan of northern Morocco. He and al-Hurra ruled from 1526 to 1545 and despite her frequent raiding, they had two sons and a daughter.

Al-Hurra's raiding flourished and soon Spain and Portugal acknowledged her as 'Pirate Queen of the Seas' and sent representatives to her court in Fez who tried to negotiate the release of Christian captives. Noble captives were held for ransom from their families, while sailors and commoners were sold in the great slave markets of the world, including Constantinople.

In 1532, el-Outassi sent overtures to King of France, Francis I (1494–1547) through trader Hémon de Molon, encouraging the French king to develop trade relations. Francis I appointed Pierre de Piton as ambassador to 'Sultan [Ahmed] el-Outassi' the following year. In a letter to King Francis I, dated 13 August 1533, el-Outassi welcomed French overtures and granted a treaty stipulating freedom of shipping and protection from pirates for French traders. However, France dithered in signing the treaty, being distracted by repeated warring conflicts with the English King Henry VIII. France did not begin sending ships to Morocco until 1555, after signing a treaty under the rule of French King Henry II (1519–1559), son of King Francis I. During this period, al-Hurra continued raiding and robbing ships in the Mediterranean.

Spanish historical documents from 1540 chronicle negotiations 'between the Spaniards and Sayyida al-Hurra' after her successful pirate raids on Gibraltar in which her pirates took 'much booty and many prisoners'.[8] Al-Hurra eventually became the main negotiator with the Spanish and Portuguese governments when they sought to free European captives held by other Barbary Coast pirates. She earned the reputation of a prudent negotiator. Despite her skilled negotiations and formidable prowess in pirating, palace intrigue was al-Hurra's downfall. After ruling with el-Outassi for thirty years, in 1542, at the age of 57, she was overthrown in a palace coup orchestrated by her family.

Al-Hurra's son-in-law Moulay Ahmed al-Hassan al-Mandri (Abou Hassan al-Mandri's grandson), anticipating the downfall of the Wattasids, allied with their tribal foes, the Saadis. Arriving with his army in 1542 in Tétouan he deposed al-Hurra.

At odds with the merchants of Tétouan, who blamed her for their loss of revenues at the hands of the Spanish and Portuguese who had opened new trade routes through the Americas, she capitulated and raised no arms in her defence. Instead, she retired (some claim she was exiled) to Chefchaouen, where she lived for almost two decades, before dying on 14 July 1561.[9]

In 1545, el-Outassi was taken prisoner by his southern rivals, the Saadians. Ali Abu Hassun, regent for al-Hurra and el-Outassi's youngest son Nasir al-Qasiri, decided to pledge allegiance to the Ottomans in order to obtain their support. After much fighting, el-Outassi's reign was restored. However, his restoration was short-lived, and civil war again plagued his kingdom. After the Battle of Tadla, the Saadi princes of Tagmadert, who had ruled southern Morocco since 1511 deposed the Wattasids in 1554.

Chapter 8

Zhèng Shí, From Flower Boats to the Red Flag Fleet

Pirate:	Zhèng Shí (meaning widow of Zhèng Yī)
Birth name:	Shi Yang
Also known as:	Ching Shih
	Shi Xiang Gu
	Shi Xianggu
	Zhèng Yī Sao (meaning wife of Zhèng Yī)
	Shek Yeung
Date of birth:	*c.*1775
Place of birth:	Unknown
Married:	Cheung Po Tsai and Zhèng Yī
Date of death:	1844
Place of death:	Unknown

Zhèng Shí was a Chinese leader of the Red Flag Fleet (also known as the Guangdong Pirate Confederation) who were active in the South China Sea from 1801 to 1810.[1]

Exporting gold to foreigners was a capital offence under the Qing dynasty, but everybody knew the wealthy Hong merchants in bustling Canton (modern-day Guangzhou) in China clandestinely sold gold to the English, French, Dutch, Danes and Swedes in order to keep their own lucrative Southeast Asian junk and inland businesses afloat.

Everyone including savvy pirates like Zhèng Shí knew Canton averaged between twenty-five to thirty-five foreign vessels a year, which left the southern China port city's thirteen 'factories' – Qing designated warehouses for Europeans of differing nations – filled to the rafters with expensive Bohea (first picking) and Suchon teas, silks, spices, porcelain and gold.

The Canton System (1757–1842)[2] regulated what nation could trade with China and which ports were open to them. As a nation, China has 11,000 miles of coastline and 6,000 islands.[3]

Only the Japanese were excluded from this trade, as they were considered *persona non grata* in Qing-dynasty Canton in 1775, by then the only Chinese port remaining open to non-Russian foreign trade. That year, Zhèng Shí was born into the floating world of Canton's Tanka flower boats and brothels in 1775 near Xinhui, Canton.[4]

Although hers was a humble beginning, by the time she was in her late twenties, she would be one of the most feared and powerful women ever to sail South Asian seas, commanding the Red Flag Fleet Guangzhou Pirate Confederation (which had approximately 400 ships and thousands of pirates in 1805). By 1810, Zhèng Shí had under her personal command no less than 24 ships and 1,433 blood-thirsty pirates.[5]

While the American Revolution was in its infancy, the great trading companies of Europe, the British East Indian Company, the Dutch East India Company, the Danish Asiatic Company, as well as the French and Swedes were robustly speculating in tea, silks, gold, spices and porcelain while amassing monstrous fortunes, if their ships made it safely to home ports. However, European wars often interfered with trade, as did the worldwide predation of prowling pirates.

Sea power fostered European imperialism during the eighteenth century. Ever avaricious monarchs exported their people and domestic products of their kingdoms, in numerous national merchant marine vessels, protected by their imposing navies.

In the main, these trading merchant vessels took goods to overseas colonies that were designed to function as closed, monopolised markets, ensuring profits for their backers who owned shares in ships and enterprises. Sea power was most pervasive wherever large warships could operate and mobilise.

Zhèng Shí was 9 years old in 1784 when the first non-military, independent American merchant ship sailed into Canton to trade. Little is known about the daily life of women in the floating, flower boat business (*Huashi*) and brothels anchored in Canton's River Pearl, but their flower boat businesses shared the same waterfront as the thirteen factories owned by Hong merchants, who rented them to foreign traders.

These factories (and the Europeans who managed them, the company factors) offered residential accommodation for visiting foreigners and doubled as storehouses for tea, porcelain, raw and finished silks and exotic spices like cloves, nutmegs and pepper, much prized by Europeans. And which brought higher prices at home and in the colonies.

The Qing Empire was threatened both internally and externally during the transition from the Qianlong era (1735 –1796) to the Jiaqing-Daoguang era (1797–1850).[6] During this period of civil turmoil and disorder, the Manchu Court was no longer as eager to maintain its domination or to be as proactive in controlling China's inner sea space as it had been previously. Eventually, the Qing perspective on the 'free seas' was sternly challenged by Western intruders, who sought to realise their aggressive, expansionist policies in East Asia.

Zhèng Shí was reportedly quite beautiful by the time she was in her late teens and she was considered by some as a much sought-after companion. She was a member of the Tanka, the 'outcast' boat people whose vessels lined Canton's Pearl River for more than 4 miles. Higher-born Chinese women were forbidden to have sexual relations with foreigners, but Tanka women often married Portuguese traders who inhabited the island of Macao, and in Canton, they served the sexual needs of foreign sailors.

Ordinary Chinese sex workers feared serving Western men as they 'looked like grisly barbarians',[7] but the outcast Tanka freely mingled with Westerners. Tanka sex workers were stereotyped by Qing government officials as greedy and arrogant, as well as being well known for mocking their clients and occasionally punching them. Qing dynasty officials publicly warned Westerners every year about the dangers they faced consorting with the Tanka. Unlike Chinese women of all classes, Tanka women did not endure the practice of foot-binding.

Nicknamed 'saltwater girls' ('*ham sui mui*' in Cantonese)[8] for their services as sex workers to foreigners, Tanka women were severely ostracised by the Canton Chinese community. Tanka women working as flower boat sex workers for foreigners also commonly kept a 'nursery' of young girls. Some were Tanka girls, while others were rescued 'rubbish heap' infants, as infanticide exposure of inconvenient baby girls was widespread.

These girls were specifically raised and trained for export. Many were sold into sex work in overseas Chinese communities in Australia and America, or the very skilled were to serve abroad ships as a foreigner's concubine. At the time, it was rumoured that Zhèng Shí was originally raised in one of these nurseries.

Tanka people, forbidden by Chinese law from 1730 to settle in villages or cities on shore or to compete at literary or civil service examinations, were from the pioneering days of the East India companies, reliable allies of foreigners. In addition to being 'pillow girls', the Tanka also furnished maritime pilots and supplies of provisions to British troopships and mercantile vessels, even during times when to do so was declared treason, punishable by death. They were the 'gofers' of the foreign factories of Canton and later of British shipping at Lintin, Kamsingmoon, Tungkin and Hongkong Bay.

American captains were often amazed by the diverse nautical skills of Tanka women who piloted their own small craft and who frequently assailed the larger foreign vessels offering to transport officers and other crewmen to their moored flower boat brothels. One American captain, who took up their offer, marvelled at the young tiller woman who navigated with a baby at her breast. He reported that Tanka women's ships were neat and tidy with several generations living aboard and all had religious altars with offerings. He was surprised to discover many Tanka flower boats were decorated with Western oddities like clocks.[9] According to historians Elizabeth Andrew and Katherine Bushnell who contemporaneously wrote about Tanka women, Tanka women could not marry the Chinese, as they were ethnically different and were descendants of the original southern China native peoples. Tanka were restricted to working and living on the waterways.

According to Dr Yvan Melchoir, who visited the Tanka people,

> As darkness downs … the flower-boats now suspend from the mast-head their gigantic lanterns, brilliantly painted with dragons entwined, and nameless blossoms; and these semi-transparent beacons serve to point out those dazzling abodes … Yet, no – it is the fair boat-woman herself who is initiating us – M. Rondot, M. Renard, and me – in a portion of the mysteries of the floating-city, and who puts it in our power to peep a little into the inner life of her order. Not unfrequently, the boats of the poor present family groups full of grace and natural simplicity; the children especially being the objects of the tenderest

> caresses. The father, who has just ceased labour, worn with fatigue, takes upon his knees the youngest of his children; he encircles the little creature with his arms, that it may not fall; and so, rice-bowl in one hand and bamboo chopsticks in the other, he feeds the babe with the soft, assiduous patience of an attentive mother.
>
> The Tanka-girls, contrary to the practice among the women of the bourgeoisie and upper ranks, eat with their husbands, it being only fair that the food won by their common labour should be partaken of in common. We felt an interest of a very attractive kind in watching these poor families at their meals. The dish of rice and fish, which constitutes the whole repast, is placed upon the deck of the vessel; the father, mother, grandfather, and grandmother are ranged all round it upon cane seats, while the children, basin in hand, edge in and take places at the corners as they can. There is laughter, there is conversation, in these rude homes, and the shadow of thoughts of privation to come falls not upon the simple feast: each one, with a cheerful heart, eats his share of the meagre reward of a day of painful toil.[10]

Under the trade restrictions imposed on foreigners at the time, foreign ships were prohibited from arranging to trade in Canton during the winter and all inbound foreign vessels had to anchor in the Whampoa Roads area southwest of Canton to await inspection by the authorities. Foreigners had to live in the area of the factories and their behaviour was under the strict control of the Hongs.

Chinese merchants were required by the government to be guarantors for every foreign trading vessel entering Canton Harbour and they were responsible for the ship's crew, captain and the supercargo – a man whose job was to oversee the disposition of the cargo and who was employed by the cargo owners. He differed from East India factors who were required to live in the factories in foreign ports, as he arrived and departed with the ship.

From 1699 to 1714, the British East India Company and the French East India Company sent a ship or two each year; while the Austrian Ostend General India Company arrived for trade in 1717, and the Dutch East India Company came in 1729. The Danish Asiatic Company sailed into Canton in 1731, and in 1732, the Swedish East India Company also arrived. The occasional Prussian or Trieste company merchant vessels joined these. The first independent American ship did not arrive until 1784 and the first colonial Australian one in 1788. By that time, Canton was one of the greatest ports in the world, organised under the strictly regimented Canton System. Primary exports were silks, porcelain and tea.[11]

Any tax payments due from a foreign trader had to be guaranteed to the government by the local merchant. Further trade restrictions prevented Chinese citizens from working for or borrowing capital from foreigners, although both practices were clandestinely widespread. Chinese citizens were also prohibited from obtaining information about European market conditions, which could lead to unfair advantages among the rich Hong merchant families.[12] This latter prohibition provided fertile grounds for lucrative 'pillow talk' information exchanges gleaned by women like Zhèng Shí who were plying their trade in the flower boats and floating brothels, which served foreigners.

It is not known whether the infamous pirate, Zhèng Yī, kidnapped Zhèng Shí or if she was sold to him. Romantics believe Zhèng Yī raided the brothel so he could marry her. What is known is the terms of her marriage contract with him. Zhèng Yī was heir to a family of rich and successful pirates who traced their piratical origins to the mid-seventeenth century. His motivation for marriage is in dispute, as some scholars argue he became infatuated with Zhèng Shí, while others believe their marriage was designed to consolidate power with the powerful Tanka clans. Zhèng Shí is believed to have agreed to lend her powers of intrigue to her husband's piracy by a formal marriage contract, which stipulated she would be an equal partner in the leadership of the pirate fleet, and that half Zhèng Yī's share of the plunder would be hers.[13]

Zhèng Yī had been previously married, and when he married Zhèng Shí, she adopted his son Cheung Po Tsai, as her stepson, therefore, making him Zhèng Yī's legal heir. During the first years of their marriage, while they were raiding at sea, Zhèng Shí gave birth to two sons, Zhèng Yīng Shí and Zhèng Xióng Shí.[14]

As a skilled pirate and unorthodox negotiator, Zhèng Yī used family connections with the corrupt military, and his fearsome reputation to bid and bind the frequently warring, disparate Cantonese pirate fleets into an alliance. Because she was Tanka, Zhèng Shí used her influence and made alliances between Zhèng Yī and the Tanka pirates. By 1804, Zhèng Yī's coalition of cutthroats had grown from 200 to 600 ships – more vessels than the Imperial Chinese Navy – with 17,000 men. Their alliances created a terrifying flotilla known all over China and the South Asian seas as the Red Flag Fleet. During the next six years, the Zhèngs built a powerful coalition of six colour coded fleets, with their own Red Flag Fleet leading their pirate armada. Subsidiary fleets included the Black, White, Blue, Yellow and Green Flag fleets.

In April 1804, the Zhèngs' fleet laid siege to and blockaded the vital, wealthy Portuguese trading port at Macau.[15] Portugal sent a battle flotilla against the pirate armada, but the Zhèngs' junks viciously defeated the unwieldy, although superiorly armed Portuguese man-of-wars.

Alarmed at the disruption to trade, Britain tried to intervene to protect its tea clippers, but did not dare take on the full might of the pirates. Instead, the British Royal Navy began providing naval escorts for British and allied shipping in the area. Both nations hired bounty hunting mercenary ships to prey on the Zhèngs' fleets.

On 16 November 1807, at the age of 39, after only six years of marriage, Zhèng Yī was killed during a junk raid off the coast of Annam (modern-day Vietnam), which was then enmeshed in the Tay Son Rebellion. At the time of his death, the Zhèngs' commanded almost 1,200 ships.[16]

Now known as Zhèng Shí (widow of Zhèng Yī), she began cementing alliances and manoeuvring her way into his leadership position. She solidified her partnership with her stepson, Cheung Po Tsai, by becoming his lover. Zhèng Shí used her legendary wiles and reputation to solidify relationships with rivals who initially were reluctant to acknowledge her authority. She sought the legitimate support from the most powerful members of Zhèng Yī's family, including his nephew Ching Pao-yang and his cousin's son Ching Ch'i. She then drew on the coalition formed by her husband by enlisting some of the fleet captains' existing loyalties to her husband and by making herself and her Tanka connections indispensable to the remaining captains. Her efforts won her authority over the Black and White Flag fleets.

With such a large and diverse fleet at her command, Cheung Po Tsai assisted in managing the consortium's and the Red Flag Fleet's day-to-day operations. However, as custom demanded a man be in charge of the fleet, Zhèng Shí officially named him captain of the Red Flag fleet. Zhèng Shí began uniting the fleets by issuing a strict, written code of maritime laws – a first in Asian piracy. Although historian Charles Fried Neumann in his book, *The History of Pirates Who Infested the China Sea: From 1807 to 1810*, claims that the code was written by Cheung Po Tsai,[17] other scholars contend Cheung Po Tsai only issued a code of three regulations (*san-t'iao*), for his own fleet, but that they were never written. Zhèng Shí is believed the code's author, which was strictly enforced.[18]

First was the stipulation that anyone giving their own orders or disobeying those of a superior was to be beheaded immediately. Second, and most pragmatically, no one was to steal from any villagers supplying the fleet. Moreover, theft from the public fund would not be tolerated. A first-time offence resulted in a severe whipping, while the withholding of large amount of booty or subsequent offences of theft from the common fund resulted in death. Third, all plundered goods must be presented to everyone for inspection and then registered with the purser, before being distributed by the fleet captain. The pirate who had plundered the goods received a 20 per cent share while the rest was allocated to the public fund for dispersal. Fourth, gold and silver coinage, and other specie was turned over to the ship's captain, who only returned a small amount to the plunderer. The remainder was used to purchase supplies for fleet ships that were less successful.

Zhèng Shí developed special rules for female captives. Previously, pirates had released or ransomed female captives. Under Zhèng Shí's code, pirates who raped women captives were condemned to death.[19]

Occasionally, pirates made their most beautiful captives their wives or concubines. If a pirate took a wife, the code ensured he had to be faithful, and the wife was treated as a member of the fleet and subject to its discipline. Girls and women deemed unattractive were often released, while others were ransomed. However, if a pirate had consensual sex with a captive, the pirate was beheaded and the woman he was with had cannonballs attached to her feet and was thrown over the side of the ship to drown.

Violations of other parts of the code were severely punished with quartering, flogging or clapping in irons depending on the offence. Deserters had their ears sliced off and were paraded before the crew. Contemporary Qing reports allege Zhèng Shí would have some offenders' feet nailed to the deck. The net result of the code was a strictly disciplined fleet that was desperate in defence, intrepid in attack and unyielding even when faced with superior numbers.[20]

Zhèng Shí was not satisfied in just re-shaping the fleet. She developed hegemony over many coastal villages, even taxing them. Her Red Flag Fleet of 300 ships pillaged towns, markets and villages that did not supply them, from Canton to Macao, much to the dismay of the Portuguese. At Sanshan village, her crews beheaded eighty men, and kidnapped the women and children, holding them for ransom. When it was not paid, she sold them into slavery.

The wife of Cheung Po Tsai's lieutenant, Cai Qian Ma, was a Western weaponry expert who spoke fluent English. Within the fleet, she was notorious for her viciousness in battle, addiction to opiates and sexual exploits. But as well as this, Cai Qian Ma was an expert negotiator. She was able to provide Zhèng Shí and Cheung Po Tsai with strong connections to Western weapon dealers – thereby supplying the fleet with British guns.[21]

Alarmed by the numerous successful raids and the loss of imperial tax revenues, in January 1808 the Chinese government tried to destroy her fleet during a series of raging battles. However, she skilfully outmanoeuvred the Imperial Chinese Navy fleet and captured sixty-three of their ships.

Thereafter, the Imperial Chinese Navy was reduced to using commandeered fishing vessels to engage the Red Flag Fleet. While the government was attacking her, Zhèng Shí faced a more perilous threat from other pirate fleets. O-po-tae, a formerly allied-pirate captain, turned his back on her and began working with the Qing government. His knowledge of Red Flag Fleet safe havens forced Zhèng Shí to retreat from the coast.

For many years, the Red Flag Fleet, under Zhèng Shí's rule, was not defeated, neither by Qing-dynasty Chinese officials nor by the British or Portuguese bounty hunters, employed by the Qing dynasty. During a daring raid in 1809, she captured Richard Glasspoole, officer of the British East India Company ship *The Marquis of Ely*, and seven British sailors.

Fortune turned her back on the Red Flag Fleet and between September 1809 and January 1810; Zhèng Shí and Cheung Po Tsai's fleet suffered a series of defeats inflicted by the Portuguese navy at the Battle of the Tiger's Mouth. Blockaded for two weeks and facing the might of the Portuguese armada, Zhèng Shí negotiated surrender, as there was no way they would be able to hold out.[22]

With the assistance of the Portuguese flotilla commander Alcoforado, the Qing government offered amnesty to all pirates who agreed to surrender, and who pledged an end their careers. The Qing allowed them to keep the loot they had amassed that year. This amnesty agreement Zhèng Shí, Cheong Po Tsai and Alcoforado negotiated with the government was on the condition that 60 pirates would be banished, and 151 would be exiled. To slate the public's thirst for revenge, only 126 would be executed. Zhèng Shí's entire fleet at the time was home to 17,318 pirates. All remaining pirates only had to surrender their weapons. As part of the deal, Cheung Po Tsai was granted an appointment as admiral of the Imperial Chinese Navy and was commissioned to hunt other pirates.[23]

After three years of bounty hunting other pirates, Zhèng Shí and her adopted son Cheung Po Tsai petitioned the governor of Canton, Zhang Bailing, to dissolve their mother and son relationship, and allow them to marry. The governor granted their petition. Zhèng Shí and Cheung Po Tsai were married with the governor himself acting as witness. In 1813, Zhèng Shí gave birth to another son. She would later give birth to her only daughter.

Nine years later, Cheung Po Tsai died while bounty hunting at sea and Zhèng Shí decided she had enough of maritime life, she wanted to retire. Moving her family back to Canton, she opened a floating brothel and gambling house on the Pearl River, which she operated until her death in 1844. Surrounded by family, having outlived two husbands and the perils of a life of piracy, she died peacefully in her own bed at an advanced age of 69.[24]

Chapter 9

Queen Teuta of the Ardiaei

Pirate:	**Queen Teuta**
Also known as:	**Queen Teuta of the Ardiaei**
Date of birth:	**Unknown**
Place of birth:	**Unknown**
Married:	**King Agron of the Ardiaei**
Reigned as regent:	**From 231 to 227 BCE**
Date of death:	**Unknown**
Place of death:	**Unknown**

'I want him dead. I want him to greet his gods while aboard his ship and not on our lands. Send our best assassins to ensure his smart mouth never utters another word of derision.' This is what Queen Teuta of the Ardiaei reportedly instructed her military adjutant.

On what should have been a glorious, celebratory day of victory, Queen Teuta seethed with anger at the disrespect this bold young Roman had defiantly heaped upon the Queen Regent of Illyria, as if she were a common peasant, unfamiliar with the laws. The arrogant man whose murder she authored, was no ordinary Roman citizen. He was, in fact, no less than one of the two Republican Roman ambassadors, the brothers Gaius and Lucius Coruncanius,[1] sent by the Roman Senate to negotiate with her. These up-and-coming young men from a staunch plebian Republican family, both had been appointed by the senate to plead with Queen Teuta to stop her pirates from harassing Roman shipping.

While not of patrician stock, the Coruncanius family was part of the new men – *novo homo* – plebians rising through the ranks of the *cursus honorum* – the ranked and titled administrative posts leading to a seat in the senate, if they or their families could afford it.

Earlier that day, Illyrian Queen Teuta had been wildly ecstatic as her fleet of piratical ships breezed into her home port of Scodra (Shkodër, Albania's fifth largest city today).

Queen Teuta was fresh from fighting the Epirotes of Epirus and their Gaulish mercenaries. Having sacked Phoenice, the Epirotes' largest maritime trading centre, her ships were heavily laden with spoils and their decks were thickly populated with slaves. The wealth she had taken from the richest maritime city in the world at the time, was nothing less than astonishing.

While some Greek historians believe that Queen Teuta had not originally intended to plunder Phoenice, as her fleet of pirate ships had stopped there to take on stores and drinking water, but some of her crews purportedly fell in with the Gauls, the 800 mercenaries the Epirotes employed to guard their cities. Mercenaries would often be purchased by the highest bidder and the Illyrians, apparently, offered the Gauls a substantial share to turn against their current benefactors. The Gauls agreed and after opening the gates of the city to the Illyrian pirates and military, they riotously joined them in its sacking.[2]

Despite this betrayal by their military mercenaries, the Epirotes regrouped and made a defensive stand by destroying a bridge over the river and ordering their troops to battle formation outside the city walls, when they learned to their horror that overland a 5,000-men strong Illyrian army was on the march and would appear shortly to engage them in battle. Terrified, the Epirotes also sent messengers to their Greek allies, the Aetolian League and the Achaean League begging their support against the Illyrian onslaught.

Undeterred, the Illyrians rebuilt the bridge overnight, crossed the river and engaged in battle the next morning at dawn, soundly beating the Epirotes and taking many slaves and prisoners. If Queen Teuta had not intended to sack Phoenicia, why would she have had an army marching on the city?

Historic authors like Polybius and Strabo often colour their retelling of her story laced with misogynistic propaganda. In the context of their times, they were writing for a predominately masculine audience of Greek and Roman patrons, not Illyrians.

As a new widow to her King Agron, and ruling as regent for her infant stepson Pinnes, Queen Teuta intended to keep pace with Agron's expansive policies. Her first administrative order was to enlarge and engage a substantial fleet of raiding ships by issuing letters of marque allowing captains to plunder all ships of any nation they came upon while plying the Adriatic and Ionian seas.

During the sacking of Phoenice, some of Queen Teuta's naval crews in cahoots with the Gauls attacked and killed Roman traders, whose bereft families appealed to the Roman Senate for redress. According to Polybius in Histories, Book 2, Number 7, the Gauls that the Epirotes employed had previously been employed by the Carthaginians, whom they also betrayed and when their Carthaginian city fell to the Roman onslaught, the Romans put the Gaulish mercenaries aboard ships and they were told never to set foot in Italy. Despite their reputation for betrayal, the Gauls sought employment by the Epirotes to protect their cities.

Previously, the Republican Roman senate, embroiled with its Carthaginian wars, had enjoyed a 'live and let live' policy with the Illyrian pirates, but this time the murder of the Roman traders by the Illyrians went a step too far and the senate appointed two ambassadors who had the ill-fortune to arrive at Scodra the same day as Queen Teuta. They asked for an audience, and it was granted.

Flush with Epirus' victory, and the treaty she and her commanders had earnestly won, and having recently put down a rebellion against her regency from her own people, Queen Teuta did not expect the Romans' dismissive and deprecating attitude. During their audience with Queen Teuta, Gaius and Lucius Coruncanius 'began to speak of the outrages committed against them.' Queen Teuta, during the whole interview, listened to them in a most arrogant and overbearing manner, and when they had finished speaking, she said she would see to it that Rome suffered no public wrong from Illyria, but that, as for private wrongs, it was contrary to the custom of Illyrians kings to hinder their subjects from winning booty from the sea.[3] 'The younger ambassador [Lucius Coruncanius] was very indignant at these words of hers, and spoke out with a frankness most proper indeed, but highly inopportune.' 'O Teuta,' Lucius Coruncanius said,

> the Romans have an admirable custom, which is to punish publicly the doers of private wrongs and publicly come to the help of the wronged. Be sure that we will try, Gods willing, by might and main and right

> soon, to force thee to mend the custom toward the Illyrians of their kings.[4]

Queen Teuta's assassin did his work well and when this diplomatic affront was realised by the Roman senate, they did not hesitate, instead they levied legions and a fleet of ships and prepared for war against Queen Teuta and the Illyrian people.

In ancient Roman times Illyria/Illyricum across the Adriatic Sea from Italy, included the area of the southeastern Adriatic Sea coast (modern-day Montenegro and Albania) and its inland rural areas, stretching between the eastern Adriatic and the River Danube.

According to Strabo who extensively travelled the ancient world and wrote about it,

> The whole Illyrian seaboard is exceedingly well supplied with harbors [*sic*], not only on the continuous coast itself but also in the neighboring [*sic*] islands, although the reverse is the case with that part of the Italian seaboard which lies opposite, since it is harbourless. But both seaboards in like manner are sunny and good for fruits, for the olive and the vine flourish there, except, perhaps, in places here or there that are utterly rugged. But although the Illyrian seaboard is such, people in earlier times made but small account of it – perhaps in part owing to their ignorance of its fertility, though mostly because of the wildness of the inhabitants and their piratical habits. But the whole of the country situated above this is mountainous, cold, and subject to snows, especially the northerly part, so that there is a scarcity of the vine, not only on the heights but also on the levels. These latter are the mountain-plains occupied by the Pannonians; on the south they extend as far as the country of the Dalmatians and the Ardiaei, on the north they end at the [River] Ister, while on the east they border on the country of the Scordisci, that is, on the country that extends along the mountains of the Macedonians and the Thracians.[5]

Broadly speaking, the Illyrians were an early European ethnic group of tribal peoples living along the Balkan peninsula. Archaically, beginning about 500 BCE the Illyrian tribes in the south, nearest Apollonia were colonised by the

Greeks. According to Aristotle, the Illyrians invited the Greeks to colonise their land, but thereafter they were treated like serfs or slaves by the Greeks in Apollonia and other cities.[6]

Wars of conquest were ubiquitous across Europe and what the ancients described as Asia or the East in the mid-second century BCE, and the Illyrian kings were like many others, but they had an advantage as they occupied miles and miles of coastline along the Adriatic Sea opposite the busy trading and Republican Roman Empire. Not only did the Illyrians live inland, but they were renowned as were a seafaring people.

King Agron, son of Pleuratus belonged to the ruling house of the Ardiaei. According to Polybius in his second-century BCE *Histories*, Book 2, Number 2, 'Agron was king of that part of Illyria which borders Adriatic Sea, over which Pyrrhus and his successors had held sway. In turn he captured part of Epirus and also Corcyra, Epidamnus and Pharos in succession, and established garrisons there.'

King Agron of the Ardiaei tribe was previously married to Queen Triteuta, who gave birth to a son they named Pinnes, a few months before he mysteriously died while celebrating a victory over the Aetolians and the relief of his allies the Medionians. Polybius relates that while celebrating his victories King Agron died of a 'pleurisy' brought on by over indulgence in food and drink, and that he only suffered for a few short days before his demise.

A few months before this celebrated victory, after his son's birth, he divorced Queen Triteuta and married Queen Teuta, then named her as regent and the boy's stepmother, just before he suddenly died. King Agron's Ardiaean kingdom was transformed into a formidable power – both at sea and on land – under his leadership. By his military conquests and coastal expansions, he consolidated his power base and became the most powerful king who ever reigned in Illyria.

Queen Teuta was juggling personal grief, restive warlords and unruly tribal leaders when she assumed the mantle of queen regent for her minor infant stepson Pinnes in 230 BCE.

Literally, Teuta means 'mistress of her people',[7] and may, in fact, be her title as understood by Roman historians rather than her actual name. Today, little is known about her early years and upbringing, however it is believed Queen Teuta was the first child of a noble Illyrian family and was born around

268 BCE. She received a traditional education but was also trained as if she was a boy, learning the art of war, hunting, horse riding, etc.[8]

As titular queen of the Ardiaean empire, Queen Teuta continued the maritime expansion founded by her husband, King Agron, who favoured profitable raiding to trading with Republican Rome. The Adriatic Sea teamed with Roman merchant vessels plying trade between Grecia Magna and other places.

According to Polybius,

> He [King Agron] was succeeded on the throne by his wife [Queen] Teuta, who left the details of administration to friends on whom she relied. As, with a woman's natural shortness of view, she could see nothing but the recent success and had no eyes for what was going on elsewhere, she in the first place gave letters of marque to privateers to pillage any ships they met, and next she collected a fleet and force of troops as large as the former one and sent it out, ordering the commanders to treat all countries alike as belonging to their enemies.[9]

Illyrians pirates were well-known raiders and feared throughout the region, as they often killed their captives, when there was no hope of holding them for ransom. The Illyrians preyed on ships of all nations and flags, especially Greek and Romans.

When Queen Teuta took the throne, she was beset by rebellious Illyrian tribal leaders seeking power, who feared she would be a weak leader. Little is known about her early years and upbringing.

Illyria much like Germania at the time was a loose confederation of disparate tribes, but the Illyrians had banded together and roamed the seas beneath the banner of the strongest tribal leader their king or queen. They were described by Herodotus as 'a peasant army led by aristocrats'.

Herodotus among others classified the Illyrians as a barbarous people, who resembled the ruder tribes of Thrace. Both tribes apparently tattooing their people and offered human sacrifices to their gods. The women of Illyria seem to have occupied a high position socially and even to have exercised political power.[10]

Aghast by the murder of their ambassador, the Romans began readying their troops to cross the Adriatic Sea and wage war. While the raiding/sailing season was with still her, Queen Teuta raised her largest fleet and began raiding other Greek cities.

Dividing her forces, Queen Teuta attacked both Corcyra and Epidamnus. At Epidamnus, her fleet professed the need for taking on water and stores, where they came upon the land dressed only in tunicas and carrying water amphorae. But in a Trojan horse-like deception, hidden inside the water jugs were their swords. They slew the gate guards, and with reinforcements from their ships, they took the greater portion of the city walls without heavy losses. The citizenry caught off guard, nevertheless made a spirited defence, and after much conflict through their undaunted courage they drove the Illyrians from the city.

Hastily, the Illyrian fleet joined their brethren in besieging the town of Corcyra, whose inhabitants appealed to the Aetolian and the Achaean leagues to support them with ships and troops. The Achaeans launched their ten-decked ships of war and fought the winds with oars all the way to Corcyra.[11]

Queen Teuta had signed a treaty of mutual assistance with the Acarnanians who manned their seven-decked warships and joined the Illyrians in rebuffing the Achaean fleet off the islands then called Paxi. Arachnidan and Achaean fleets fought without victory for either, with only their crews wounded. But the Illyrians lashed their galleys four abreast and disregarding their imminent peril they attacked the enemy by throwing their four-ships as one athwart the enemy's galleys. Once entangled, the Illyrians in true piratical tradition boarded the Achaean vessels.

Superior Illyrian numbers of troops led to the Achaean League's defeat – the Illyrians taking four triremes and sinking one quinquereme with all hands lost, including Margos of Caryneia, who has sailed his entire life with the Achaean League. The supporters of the Acarnanian's watching the victory by the Illyrian's, turned tail and set sail for their home port, leaving the Acarnanians in the lurch. Such were Queen Teuta's victories, as recorded by her enemies.

The Corycreans made peace and signed a pact with the Illyrians after a short siege. Once the fighting was over at Corcyra, the Illyrian admirals set sail for Epidamnus.

Meanwhile, Republican Rome under consuls Aulus Postumius and Gnaeus Fulvius (Marc Antony's first wife Fulvia would later be born into this distinguished family), had amassed 200 war ships and land forces for what historians would later call the First Illyrian War. Fulvius intended to sail direct to Corcyra, as he thought the siege was still underway, but when he discovered it was lifted, he proceeded there anyway in order to learn the truth of what had taken place, and to test the truthfulness of offers made by Demetrius.

Demetrius, a tribal warlord (also known as King of Pharos), was at odds with Queen Teuta, and fearing her military prowess, he offered Rome all the assistance he could provide them; if they would ensure his safety and that of his people, he would act as a client king, should Rome topple Queen Teuta and reinstate him.

Delighted by the arrival of the Romans, the Corycreans not only surrendered their garrison to them, but with the consent of Demetrius they also committed themselves to Roman protection. Believing this was the only way they could have lasting protection against the predations of the Illyrians, was by allying with Rome. As Roman consul, Fulvius gladly accepted their offer, declaring the Corycreans 'Friends of Rome' as he sailed for Apollonia in the south with Demetrius as the Roman guide for the rest of the campaign.

Meanwhile, Queen Teuta had her hands full with her troops blockading a rebellious uprising spawned by Demetrius at Issa, while her other forces besieged Epidamnus. Now, the second Roman consul, Aulus Postumius, embarked his army from Brundisium with 4 legions of infantry, 20,000 men and 2,000 allied horse heading for a rendezvous with Fulvius at Apollonia. At Apollonia, the Greek Strategos asked for Roman protection, and it was granted. Fulvius and Postumius then took their troops and turned toward Epidamnus, which was still besieged by the Illyrians. When the Illyrians learned the superior Roman forces were heading for the besieged city, they broke the siege and fled. The Romans took the Epidamnians under their protection and advanced afoot into the interior of Illyricum, subduing the Ardiaei who were vastly outnumbered.

Strabo, a Greek historian and philosopher, in his authoritative *Geographica*, first published in 7 BCE and last printed during his lifetime in 23 CE wrote,[12]

> The Ardiaei were called by the men of later times 'Vardiaei', because they pestered the sea through their piratical bands, the Romans pushed them back from it into the interior and forced them to till the soil. But

> the country is rough and poor and not suited to a farming population, and therefore the tribe has been utterly ruined and in fact has almost been obliterated. And this is what befell the rest of the peoples in that part of the world; for those who were most powerful in earlier times were utterly humbled or were obliterated, as, for example, among the Galatae the Boii and the Scordistae, and among the Illyrians the Autariatae, Ardiaei, and Dardanii, and among the Thracians the Triballi; that is, they were reduced in warfare by one another at first and then later by the Macedonians and the Romans.[13]

As the Romans fought the Illyrians inland, they were met on the march by envoys of several tribes who offered unconditional surrender, if Rome would offer them protection from the piratical Illyrians. Both the Partheni and the Atintanes tribes capitulated in this way and their acquiescence was accepted by the Romans.[14]

The consuls then marched their troops to Issa. Of the Illyrians troops still fighting there the Pharos troops were spared by Rome as a favour to Demetrius, while all the rest being outnumbered scattered, many fleeing to Arbo.

Realising that the writing was on the wall, Queen Teuta and a handful of her retainers sought sanctuary in Rhizon, then a small, heavily fortified and garrisoned town along the River Rhizon.

Having accomplished Queen Teuta's defeat, the Roman consuls installed Demetrius as satrap of Illyria with all rights, while they took their ships and troops to Epidamnus.[15]

Fulvius sailed back to Rome with the stories of victory while Postumius collected forty ships and with a legion he wintered there providing protection to all the tribes that were now under Rome's protection.

At the end of winter the following year[16], in fear for her life and that of her stepson, Queen Teuta sent envoys to Rome and concluded a lop-sided treaty. She was forced to pay a fixed tribute and to abandon all Illyricum, with the exception of a few small land holdings. Furthermore, as a nod to the Achaean League and the Aetolian, Rome's treaty demanded that she would not sail beyond Issus with more than two galleys and those must never bear arms. Demetrius of Pharos, her former commander would become the client king of Illyria in service of the Romans.

As consul, Postumius then sent *legates* to Greece with copies of the treaty. Not long after, Demetrius became the regent for Pinnes, and Queen Teuta disappears from history, although there is one unconfirmed report of her suicide.

Historian Leman Altuntaş believes that Queen Teuta committed suicide by jumping off a cliff in the Bay of Kotor, in modern-day Risan, Montenegro: 'According to legend, Risan was cursed by the queen's passing and is now the only town in the area without a maritime heritage. However, the exact circumstances surrounding [Queen] Teuta's death have never been confirmed.'[17]

Chapter 10

Lady Elizabeth Killigrew, All in the Family

Pirate:	**Lady Elizabeth Killigrew**
Birth name:	**Elizabeth Trewinnard/Trewynnard**
Date of birth:	**1520?**
Place of birth:	**St Erth, Cornwall, England**
Married:	**Captain Sir John Killigrew III**
Date of death:	**1585**
Place of death:	**St Budock, Cornwall, England**

Elizabeth Trewynnard (sometimes spelt Trewinnard)[1] married the ambitious, Captain John Killigrew III (*c*.1500–1526, November 1567)[2] of Arwenack, Cornwall, who was at least twenty to twenty-five years her senior. She was the daughter of John Trewynnard of Trewinnard (in Cornwall) and his unnamed first wife. Killigrew III was the son of Lady Jane Maude Killigrew (née Petit) and John Killigrew II of Arwenack.

In 1542, Captain John Killigrew III was awarded control of Cornwall shipping under royal licence by the then ailing King Henry VIII. Under the guise of legitimate taxation, Captain Sir John Killigrew III (now a knight of the realm) assembled a fleet of ships that preyed and plundered shipping in his coastal area.

He and Lady Elizabeth fortified his castle with the spoils, and when he abruptly died in 1567, Lady Elizabeth took command of his pirate crews, and with her family she continued plundering. After seizing a Spanish ship in Falmouth in 1582, Lady Elizabeth was arrested for piracy and condemned to death, but Queen Elizabeth I, having a penchant for 'pirates of the crown' pardoned her.

During the 1540s, King Henry VIII built Pendennis Castle,[3] paying rent on part of the Arwenack estate belonging to the Killigrew family. Captain Sir John Killigrew III was appointed by the king as the first hereditary governor of Pendennis Castle and after his death Queen Elizabeth I appointed as second governor his son (now) Sir John Killigrew IV (1547–1605). This lucrative governorship allowed control over all the shipping along the coasts and in the Carrick Roads harbour, then the third largest natural harbour in the world.

The governor of Pendennis Castle was a military officer's appointment. As governor Captain Sir John Killigrew III commanded the fortifications at Pendennis Castle, part of the defences of the Carrick Roads and the River Fal on the south coast of Cornwall near Falmouth. Originally fortified under King Henry VIII, defences in the area were intermittently maintained until after the Second World War (1939–1945).[4]

Pendennis Castle formed part of King Henry VIII's Device Programme and was erected between 1540 and 1542 to protect against invasion from France and the Holy Roman Empire and defended the Carrick Roads an estuary at the mouth of the River Fal. The original circular keep and gun platform was expanded at the end of the century to add additional armaments with the increasing Spanish threat, and a ring of extensive stone bastions and ramparts were built around the older castle. *Penn Dinas* in Welsh translates as headlands fortification.[5]

During King Henry VIII's reign, he devised a programme to build a number of artillery fortifications (known as the Device Forts or Device Fortifications) to defend the coasts of England and Wales. (These Device Forts were also known as Henrician castles and blockhouses.) Prior to this, the defence of the coasts had been the responsibility of the local lords, but as there were threats from the French, the Holy Roman Empire and the Spanish of possible invasions, Henry VIII issued an order (known as a device) for this programme of vast fortifications to be built as soon as possible in order to defend his country from attack. This programme of works took place between 1539 and 1547.[6] Device Forts ranged from large stone castles protecting the Downs and anchorage in Kent, to small blockhouses overlooking the entrance to Milford Haven in Pembrokeshire, and earthen bulwarks along the Essex coast line.

While some forts operated independently, others were designed to be mutually reinforcing. The Device Programme was hugely expensive, costing the Crown a total of £376,000 (estimated at between £2 billion and £82 billion in today's money).[7]

These castles were commanded by captains appointed by the Crown, overseeing small garrisons of professional gunners who operated the artillery and soldiers, who could be supplemented by the local militia in an emergency.

Lady Elizabeth and Captain Sir John Killigrew III were well equipped for fighting and defending their castle and they had ample manpower for preying upon ships that plied their waters and elsewhere. They were ambitious, often using their lands to hide their plunder.

Captain Sir John Killigrew III's trafficking with pirates had been known to the authorities since 1552, and in 1565 commissioners were appointed to undertake a formal enquiry.[8] The Killigrews developed a dubious reputation, especially in the sixteenth century as they became renowned for buccaneering. They also had a penchant for illuminating 'false lights' (lanterns placed at night atop high landmarks that lured ships into less than sailable waters). The Killigrews had a fondness for wrecking any valuable ships that visited shores close to their Arwenack estate. But behind every proud, mad or bad man in the Killigrew family, there was a determined, clever woman.[9]

Elizabeth Trewinnard married Captain Sir John Killigrew III of Arwenack around 1534. She was fertile and he was not too busy, and they had ten children, including John IV, Peter, Thomas, Henry, William, Jane, Grace, Amy, Alice and Margaret. Originally from St Erth, Lady Elizabeth became mistress of the newly built Arwenack House late in their marriage in 1567.[10] While most of this fine manor house was destroyed by fire during the English Civil War (1642–1651), parts of this fine manor house still stand today.

Some of their children would continue their parent's tradition in raiding Spanish ships ostensibly for the Crown.

According to historian John Vivian, writing in 1989,

> The Killigrews pounced like vultures on every ship that stranded on their estates, claiming the justification of ancient privilege for their actions. This example was readily followed by the common people, who could at least plead the excuse of poverty for their misdeeds.[11]

Apparently, as mistress of the manor, Lady Elizabeth took charge of the stolen goods when they reached Arwenack House. Much of their booty was thought to have been fenced locally, while some was buried on their lands and in their gardens. When criminal charges were laid against them, most were quickly dropped as the Killigrews had many powerful relatives in Parliament and at the Royal Court.

Piracy became a family affair when their eldest son Sir John Killigrew IV and his wife Mary Wolverston (*c.*1525–*c.*1587)[12] of Woolverstone Hall, Suffolk joined them. Mary was the daughter of the 'gentleman pirate' Philip Wolverston. Mary was the widow of Sir Henry Knyvett, although there is not much reference to their marriage and some people believe that Mary was, in fact, married to Sir Thomas Knyvett. There is also reference to a possible son from her first marriage who may also have become a pirate.

Mary and her husband paid large fees to officials, bribing them to allow their illicit activities. Mary played an active role in piracy, and according to some enjoyed the adventure more than her husband.[13] They had five children, John V (who would become Sir John Killigrew V), Thomas, Simon, Mary and Katherine.

According to Parliamentary records, the Killigrews – father and son – opposed Queen Mary I, and were using their ships to keep the émigrés in the Normandy ports in touch with English affairs, while they went about attacking Spanish vessels in the Channel. Father and son were both put into 'The Fleet' (Fleet Street Prison) on 28 June 1556 'to be kept there apart in close prison', and were lucky to be released three weeks later, after intercessions by their relations.

Back in favour under Queen Elizabeth I, Sir John Killigrew IV was put on the commission of the peace during his father's lifetime, but after succeeding to his estates in 1568, he became a leading and notorious figure in the county, indulging in cattle theft, and 'evil usage in keeping of a castle' and 'abuses' over arranging the quarter sessions.

Sir John Killigrew IV's speciality, however, was using his office of piracy commissioner to maintain and trade with the pirates and smugglers who frequented the coast he could so easily control from Arwenack House and Pendennis Castle. His estates covered a large part of the Falmouth area, and he owned the fee farm of Penryn borough, so there was likewise no difficulty in his being returned to Parliament when he wished.[14] Sir John Killigrew IV was not mentioned directly or indirectly in the known proceedings of the House of Commons, and we can only speculate on his motives for being elected.

The Killigrews' trafficking with the pirates had been known to the authorities since 1552, and in 1565 commissioners were appointed to undertake a formal investigation. But the senior Killigrew was powerful enough locally to evade the allegations against him. Lady Elizabeth's husband died suddenly in 1567.

Between 1575 and 1576 the Council wrote to Sir John Killigrew IV repeatedly about such matters as his imprisoning a French merchant and seizing four ships from Flushing. Even the good Earl of Bedford complained that 'the castle in Mr. Killigrew's [Sir John Killigrew IV] charge is much decayed and almost unserviceable'. Only once, in January 1569, does a commendation of his behaviour appear in the records, after he and Sir Arthur Champernowne had seized some Spanish silver and conveyed it to the Tower of London.

Parliamentary historians believe that Sir John Killigrew IV's appointment as a piracy commissioner is anomalous even by Elizabethan standards. He was a member of Parliament three times for two different ridings. The first date found for his acting as piracy commissioner although he may have been appointed earlier is in summer 1577 when he fought a duel with Vice Admiral Ambrose Digby over a local quarrel and repeated disturbance of the peace by Sir John Killigrew IV. This dispute went to arbitration by Bedford, who awarded Digby £100, which was still unpaid in December 1579.[15]

In January 1582, Sir John Killigrew IV seized a Spanish ship sheltering in Falmouth under stress of weather. After overpowering the crew, Sir John Killigrew IV seized the cargo of Holland cloth, took the ship and had it sailed to Ireland. As piracy commissioner he sent up a tendentious report and then disappeared from view. An investigation by Richard Grenville II and Edmund Tremayne disclosed that Lady Elizabeth had presented several lengths of cloth to her servants and that a daughter (or daughter-in-law) of the family had paid a debt with 20 yards of the material. Sir John Killigrew IV was summoned to attend before the Privy Council, but no details have survived in the parliamentary record of any further punishment.[16]

In January 1582, Sir John Killigrew IV's wife, Mary Wolverston (now Lady Mary Killigrew), by then in her sixties, heard a rumour that there was treasure aboard the Spanish ship *Marie of San Sebastian* anchored opposite Arwenack House, and she sent her servants to seize the ship and search the cargo. She was arrested for having received and fenced stolen goods after the seizure of

Marie of San Sebastian during which a factor was murdered when the ship was boarded by her raiding party.[17] Other family members were included in the accusation. Mary Wolverston was brought to trial and sentenced to death. Though two of her assistants were executed, she eventually received a pardon from Queen Elizabeth I. Mary's son secured her release from prison after having paid substantial bribes.[18]

According to Parliamentary records, less than a year after his mother Lady Elizabeth died, Sir John Killigrew IV died intestate on 5 March 1584, leaving numerous unpaid debts to his brother, parliamentarian Henry Killigrew, on whom he had been financially dependent for many years. He was buried at Budock.[19, 20]

Chapter 11

Christina Anna Skytte, Brothers, Sisters and Lovers

Pirate:	**Christina Anna Skytte**
Also known as:	**Anna Drake**
	Christinia Anna Drake
	Anna Skytte
Date of birth:	**9 November 1643**
Place of birth:	**Sweden**
Married:	**Gustav Drake**
Date of death:	**1 January 1677**
Place of death:	**Hagelsrum, Sweden**

'[Christina] Anna Skytte participated in the guise of a female warrior in all sorts of blood-thirsty piratical acts before her marriage to Gustaf Drake.' This was claimed by famed historian Gustaf Volmar Sylvander in his extensive history, *Kalmar stads och slotts* historia,[1] published in 1865.[2]

Born in the parish of Ålems at Mönsterås in Kalmar County, Sweden in winter 1643, Skytte was the blonde and blue-eyed daughter of *Friherre* (Baron) Jacob Skytte (*c*.1613/1616–1654) of Duderhof, Sweden and Anna Skytte (née Bielkenstjerna) (*c*.1617–1663); also, granddaughter of governor Johan Skytte (1577–1645) and niece of poet Vendela Skytte (1608–1629). She was 2 years old when her father, who was a university rector, followed in his father's footsteps and became the governor of Östergötland, a traditional southern Swedish province.

Little is known about Skytte's early years other than she received an education commensurate with their newly ennobled standing and her family's soaring fortunes.

Gustav Adolf Skytte (1637–1663), Skytte's university educated older brother, who had prestigiously served with distinction in the military, led a double life as a gentlemanly, landed aristocrat and surreptitious, blood-thirsty pirate. Three years after their father's death in 1657, Gustav Adolf Skytte, aged 20, began preying on merchant vessels in the Baltic Sea. His right-hand man was Skytte's soon-to-be husband Gustaf Drake (1634–1684) (and some historians also believe that Erik Bragge was part of the ship's crew). Unconventionally for the times, Skytte often sailed with the crew aboard her brother's ship.

Skytte was the daughter of a well-known and very famous Swedish family. Her grandfather, Johan Skytte, was born in Nyköping, Sweden in 1577, and was a well-known Swedish politician. He was son of the mayor of Nyköping, Bengt Nilsson Skräddare (*c.*1550–*c.*1602) and his first wife Anna Andersdotter (*c.*1560–*c.*1586), who was the daughter of mayor Anders Persson and his wife Elin Larsdotter.[3] (Note that Anna Andersdotter's surname appears to be a combination of her parents' surnames; Johan later adopted the surname Skytte.) Skytte's grandfather, Johan, attended school in his hometown, as well as in Stockholm and for nine years he attended foreign universities. In 1598, he earned a master's degree in philosophy at the University of Marburg in Germany.[4]

On his return from his foreign studies, in 1602, he was hired by the royal family of Sweden as a tutor for the young Prince Gustavus Adolphus, the future king. Johan Skytte was ennobled *friherre* (baron) the following year, taking the name Skytte after an extinct noble family from which he claimed descent on the maternal side.[5] Skytte's grandfather was sent to London in 1610 on a diplomatic mission, in an attempt to seek the hand of Elizabeth Stuart, the daughter of King James I (1566–1625) (also known as King James VI of Scotland), for Prince Gustav. King Gustav Adolph II (as he became) was Johan's patron.

In 1611, he was made governor of Vestmanna. Later in 1617, he was appointed a high councillor becoming a member of the Swedish Privy Council and in 1622 he was named chancellor of Uppsala Universitet (university), a post he held until his death. Johan Skytte participated in drafting the Coronation Oath of King Gustav Adolf II in 1617.[6]

In 1624, having been created a *friherre*, he was granted the barony of Tuutarhovi in Ingria, Livonia, which had just been added to the Swedish realm.

In furtherance of his career, in 1629 he was appointed governor general of Livonia, Ingria and Karelia, where he served for six years. In 1632, he was appointed chancellor of the new Academia Gustaviana (University of Tartu), in addition to his Uppsala chancellorship.

Undaunted by his scholastic responsibilities, as an appointed judge he also laid plans for a new *appellate* (appeal) court in Tartu (now in Estonia). In 1632, Skytte returned from Livonia to Uppsala and to the delight of his family. His fortunes rose again in 1634, when he was appointed to the presidency of the Göta Hovrätt *appellate* court in Jönköping.[7] He was appointed chancellor of Uppsala Universitet in 1632 having, in 1622, donated (endowed a chair, as we would say today) the Skyttean professorship of eloquence and government to the university.

His own house in Uppsala, the originally medieval building is called the Skytteanum, still exists today.[8] He married Maria Nääf Till Grönsöö, and had several children, among them Skytte's father Jacob Skytte, who as an adult lived in Duderhof.

Following in his illustrious father's footsteps, Skytte's father, Jacob, became a university rector and later governor of Osterland. He was married to Anna Bielkenstjerna. They had seven children, Jakob, Johan, Maria, Gunnilla, Gustav, Christina Anna and Sofia Beata. Skytte's older brother Gustav Adolf was born in Uppsala and attended university in 1647. He was a master of the horse in the Småland cavalry regiment from 1657 to 1658.[9]

Skytte was also the niece of the celebrated poet and aristocratic, literary salonist Vendela Skytte. Skytte's cousin was also the scandalous Maria Skytte. Unconventionally, Maria a baroness, was publicly convicted by the high court of the crime of wearing men's clothing and living openly with a married man, her master of the horse. In court, Maria's master of the horse, Count Gustaf Adam Banér, swore he had not had *coitus* – carnal relations – with her, but was exiled nonetheless for six years.

After the death of his first wife, Baroness Maria and Banér married but the courts claimed the marriage was invalid. Eventually, they managed to have their marriage legalised, but the cost to their personal reputations was irreparable.[10]

At the time of Skytte's birth, the Thirty Years' War (1618–1648) was slowly coming to its conclusion. Among southern Europeans, Sweden seemed the daunting far north. A savage land besieged by cold weather.

Politician and Catholic cleric Juan Palafox y Mendoza, a Portuguese politician, and contemporary of Skytte's times wrote, 'What will you find in Sweden and Norway except obscurity and darkness, all [are] heretics, idolators, sorcerers, poor, miserable, without order nor the use of human reason, sterile lands, and [people] living in the hills like savage beasts.'[11]

Portugal rebelled for its freedom and won it from the Spanish Hapsburgs in 1640, but the newly independent regime was shunned by most European nations, with the exception Sweden. As the Thirty Years' War still raged, Spain continued to embargo its enemies maritime trade, and so Dutch merchants turned to friendly Swedish waters for transport and trade.

In 1640, Sweden was under the able regency of Axel Gustafsson Oxenstierna (1583–1654), who as *de facto* leader ruled for the 16-year-old Queen Christina (1626–1689). Queen Christina's father King Gustav Adolph II had grand visions for Sweden and had embarked upon territorial expansions. He amassed a fine navy and trained fearsome Swedish troops that often were sold as mercenaries in the wars that swept European nations. King Gustav Adolph II, 38, would never see his expansionist dreams realised as he died on the battlefield, in Lützen, Germany. However, his stalwart troops won victory the day they lost their king.

Queen Christina was only 6 years old in 1632 when the Swedish Crown was placed upon her head. Ten years later, despite her staunch Lutheranism, Queen Christina welcomed the new Portuguese nation as an ally and as an enemy on Catholic Spain's doorstep. Freed from the Spanish yoke, the new Portuguese ambassador at her Court won a treaty with Queen Christina, bartering Sweden's plentiful timber, wool, iron and copper supplies for Iberian salt and spices.

But under the new regime, Portugal refused to grant trade access to its foreign colonies in the far east (Macao and Chinese trade ports like Hong Kong) and its colony in Brazil. Nonetheless, both sides were pleased with the agreement. Portugal was short of copper, necessary for the making of small change bronze coins, and artillery, as well as the constant need for copper kettle and vessels, necessities needed in the production of sugar in Portugal's vast sugar plantations in her Brazilian colony.

Dutch merchant and military ships were embargoed by the Spanish between 1598 and 1607, and again from 1621 to 1647.[12] In the 100 years between 1557 and 1667, 96,034 registered ships passed eastwards through the Baltic Sound; 8,700 of those ships had come from Portugal, and 78 per cent of them were carrying salt.[13]

At the time, Sweden consumed 70,000 to 80,000 barrels of salt annually. Much of it carried by Dutch vessels except during the embargo periods, when the Dutch flagged ships were replaced by the English, Danish and Hamburg shippers. Salt was vital to the fishing industry in Sweden's north.[14]

Portuguese ambassador Rodrigo de Sousa Coutinho, 1st Count of Linhares (1755–1812) returned to Lisbon with Swedish armaments. He was accompanied by Lars Skytte, a member of Christina Skytte's family, perhaps, who remained in Lisbon as Sweden's representative, giving the new Portuguese government the veneer of legitimacy.

After Oxenstierna's death and Queen Christina's sudden relinquishment of the Crown to retire in Rome, King Charles Gustav X assumed the Crown and immediately joined his actively engaged troops in Poland. His absence led King of Denmark and Norway, Frederick III, to attempt to retake lands taken from him in 1645 and he invaded Sweden. And so began the first Dano-Swedish War (1657–1658).[15]

King Charles Gustav X withdrew from Poland and moved against Denmark. However, a brutally harsh winter forced the Dano-Norwegian fleet into port and froze the Danish Great Belt and Little Belt straits. After entering Jutland from the south, King Charles Gustav X and his Swedish army of 7,000 battle-hardened veterans marched across the frozen Little Belt onto the Danish island Funen.

On 30 January 1658, the Swedes captured Funen and a few days later they captured the islands of Falster, Langeland and Lolland. Continuing onto Zealand, the Swedish army threatened Copenhagen, the Danish capital.

During this brutally harsh winter, the rapid Swedish attack across the frozen Great Belt and Little Belt straits caught Frederick III completely by surprise. He mused meeting personally with the Swedish army in battle but was dissuaded by his councillors. Instead, he offered Charles Gustav X treaty terms and after negotiations the punitive Treaty of Roskilde was signed 26 February 1658.

Sweden had won its most prestigious victory, and Denmark-Norway had suffered its worst defeat.[16] Denmark-Norway gave to Sweden the Danish provinces of Blekinge, Scania and Halland, and the island of Bornholm and the Norwegian provinces of Trondhjemlen and Bohuslen. Halland had already been under Swedish control since the signing of the Treaty of

Brömsebro in 1645, under the Treaty of Roskilde it became Swedish territory permanently.

It was during these unsettling times both at home and abroad that Christina Skytte's older brother Gustav Adolf Skytte began his piratical raids. As a teen, together with her fiancé Gustaf Drake, Christina Skytte became a partner in her brother's raiding and plundering.

Presumably, unknown to his bride's family, on 9 February 1659, Gustav Adolf Skytte[17] married Brita Margaretha (also known as Margaretta) Hamilton (?–1666),[18] daughter of Hugh (also known as Hugo) Hamilton (*c.*1607–1678)[19] of Dalserf in Scotland and Margaretha Hamilton (née Forrat) (1624–1653),[20] so she was from a good Scots family.

According to legal sources, in 1657, Skytte hired a Dutch ship together with some friends. Once at sea, Gustav Adolf Skytte murdered the captain (possibly Erik Bragge) and took over the ship, which they used in attacking ships in the Baltic Sea. They forced the small crew to swear allegiance to them. Gustav Adolf Skytte used the captain's seal and signed a document forging the ship's ownership to himself. One of his colleagues was his future brother-in-law Gustaf Drake. His sister Christina Anna Skytte was also reportedly involved. When one of their accomplices wanted to stop plundering, allegedly Christina Anna Skytte and Drake had him killed. Their pirate refuge was in Blekinge, Sweden. Whether or not Skytte infamously ordered his death is one of the questions left to history. The truth of this story remains unknown, and her culpability in the murder was not included among the legal records.

Skytte had operated in the Baltic Sea, especially around Öland according to later testimony by his captured crew since 1657, but now he and Drake decided to extend their plundering business to the Kattegatt and embarked on Gustav Adolf Skytte's ship and headed toward the Gothenburg archipelago.

Although accounts of their last act of piracy differ, it is believed that heavy storms and sickness among the crew forced them to sail back to the Baltic Sound. Here they caught sight of a Dutch ship, which was on its way from Amsterdam to Norrköping, which was later found wrecked but laden with salt, herring, wine and spices. Both Skytte and Drake agreed to plunder it.[21] Anchored at Bornholm, they set sail and chased the ship. With his fifteen-man crew, they cast lots as to who would board the Dutch vessel first. Skytte and Drake were reported to be quite drunk.[22]

After they stormed the ship, they gunned down the defenceless crewmen, who were lowered into the sea with stones tied to their feet. Their preference in pirating was to kill the crews and leave no witnesses. The Dutch ship was plundered and holed ineffectually for sinking, then the pirates continued up Kalmar County, near where Skytte and Drake disembarked. The cargo was hidden partly on the island of Blå Jungfrun and partly on Skytte's property Strömserum on the coast of Småland.[23]

One August night in 1662, the wreck was discovered by the Dutch boyar drifting towards the coast of Öland. It was suspected that an act of robbery had been committed, and rumours spread that implicated Christina Anna Skytte and Drake as the criminals.[24]

According to historian Anders Fryxell in his *Berättelser ur svenska historien*, published in 1846,[25] Gustaf Adolph Skytte then, apparently, used the murdered captain's seal to generate a false title deed to the yacht. One of the accomplices (possibly the captain or crewman of Skytte's vessel), who threatened to reveal what had happened was then allegedly subsequently murdered by Christina Anna Skytte and her brother.[26]

The Dutch envoy in Stockholm, Nicolaus Heinsius, issued a sharp note to the Swedish government, demanding strict measures against these dangerous pirates. The government gave the governors in the coastal areas orders to keep a sharp lookout and arrest warrants were issued for Drake and his crewmen.[27]

Gustav Adolf Skytte and five accomplice crewmen were arrested, investigated at Kalmar County's commissioner's court and then they were bound over and appeared before the Göta Hovrätt *appellate* court. Even though a noble, Gustav Adolf Skytte was stripped of all his properties in Sweden as were the others, and he was sentenced to death and executed in 1663, aged only 26.[28] Nobly born and a former military officer, Gustav Adolf Skytte was executed by firing squad, seen as a 'soldier's death', on 27 April 1663. His father-in-law had vainly sought clemency for his daughter's wayward husband.[29]

Avoiding the firing squad, Drake who had been a cavalry captain, and Christina Anna Skytte hastily married and managed to escape first to Prussia and then to Denmark. When he did not appear on summons, Drake was sentenced 'in absentia'.

Being a married woman and, therefore, under the responsibility of her husband, as a minor in contemporary law, Christina Anna Skytte could not be personally prosecuted, but Gustaf Drake her husband was charged in his absence and sentenced to the confiscation of his property.

After five years in exile, in 1668, the couple bravely returned to Sweden. Gustaf Drake was promptly tried for piracy in Gothenburg, but his sentence was surprising lenient. He was required to pay a fine of 1,000 (local currency) to the Court and another fine of 4,000 for the damage to the Dutch ship. He had to atone for his piracy. Thereafter, the couple went no more 'a-roving' and settled at Edeby gård in the parish of Ripsa at Nyköping in Södermanland.

In June 1665, this verdict by the Göta Hovrätt *appellate* court caused a stir in the capital and the government questioned the leniency of the verdict and the 'unjustifiable neglect and carelessness of the [*appellate*] court's [handling of the case]' and the government fined the *appellate* court the 1,000 (local currency). Gustaf Drake paid them (which should have gone to the judge's wages) and the Crown forced the *appellate* court to pay the fine to the church.

The government decided that Gustaf Drake and his wife, Christina Anna Skytte had financially suffered enough, but morally they were still outcast. The government wanted to 'let this come to your conscience and be defended before God'. The government declared Drake 'in disgrace' and forbid him and Skytte to 'stay in the places and places where we personally stay'.[30]

But Gustaf Drake was undeterred and on 19 August 1668, Drake asked the Crown for a pardon for his crime while still a juvenile and based on the services his family had provided the monarchy in the past.

In September 1668, the Crown took them 'into its favour and granted a full pardon, allowing him to present himself and [the *appellate*] court as soon as possible, whereby his crime shall be completely forgiven'. Skytte and Drake thereafter lived as well-to-do landowners. In addition to his inherited estates, Hagelsrum and Ekenäs, in Kalmar County, Drake acquired Hovby, Västra Eneby sn and Högsrum in Kalmar County. Kalmarsnäs in Uppland, which had belonged to Christina Anna Skytte, was sold to pay the fines and damages.[31]

Christina Anna Skytte lived the rest of her life at the Drake family estate of Hagelsrum in Småland. They had two children; however, only their son, Gustaf Jr., survived into adulthood. Christina Anna Skytte died on 21 January 1677 of unknown causes. She was 33.

Recent scholarship has questioned Skytte's role in the raids of her brother and her husband. Rudolf Thunander, in his detailed survey of the Göta

Hovrätt *appellate* court legal records, which led to the damning judgement on Gustav Adolf Skytte – and later Drake's acquittal – found no supporting testimony or evidence that Christina Anna Skytte had been participating in either of the two documented cases of piracy in 1657 and 1661, or in any other case of piracy.

Thunander's investigations do reveal documentary evidence that Christina Anna Skytte may have stolen her brother's seal and generated a false letter, dated 2 September 1662, in which he shouldered all of the blame for the attack on the Dutch vessel and, thus, relieved Gustaf Drake of any responsibility and acquitted him of any involvement in the enterprise.[32]

Chapter 12

Jeanne de Clisson, The Lioness of Brittany

Pirate:	**Jeanne de Clisson**
Birth name:	**Jeanne-Louise de Belleville**
Full name:	**Jeanne-Louise de Belleville, de Clisson, Dame de Montaigu**
Also known as:	**Jean/Jeanne/Jeanne-Louise Bentley**
	Jean/Jeanne de Belleville
	Jean/Jeanne/Jeanne-Louise de Châteaubriant
	Jean/Jeanne-Louise de Clisson
	Jean/Jeanne/Jeanne-Louise de Penthièvre
	The Lioness of Brittany
Date of birth:	**1300**
Place of birth:	**Brittany, France**
Married:	**Walter Bentley**
	Geoffrey de Châteaubriant VIII
	Olivier de Clisson IV
	Guy de Penthièvre
Date of death:	**1360**
Place of death:	**Les Halles, Paris, France**
Ship:	***My Revenge***

Jeanne de Clisson, also known as The Lioness of Brittany, terrorised the seas as a pirate for thirteen years. Born Jeanne-Louise de Belleville in 1300, she was the daughter of a British aristocratic family who lived in Brittany.

In 1330, she married a wealthy nobleman, Olivier de Clisson IV, who was soon ordered by the King of France to defend Brittany from the intermittent assaults by the English. After failing to defend Vannes, he was accused of defecting to the English. In 1343, he was captured, taken to Paris and executed for treason on the orders of King Philip VI.

Anne Bonny. (Digitised by the author)

Anne Bonny. (Public domain)

Above: Anne Bonny and Mary Read. (Public domain)

Left: Jack Rackham. (Public domain)

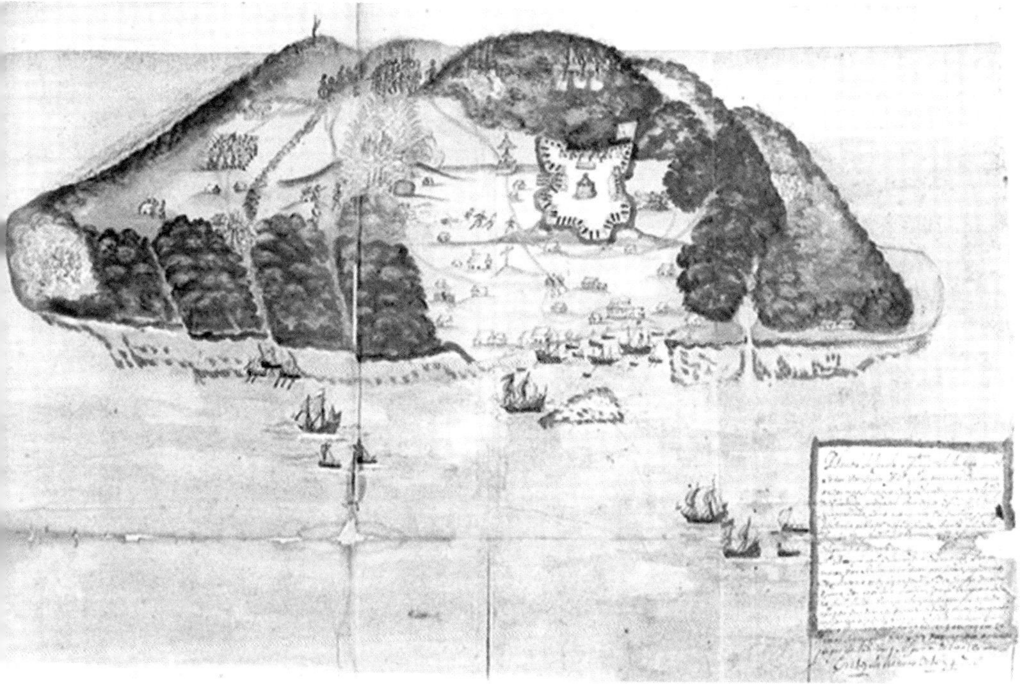

Above: Map of Tortuga. (Instituto Hidrografico de la Marina/la Roca (1654))

Right: Gráinne O'Malley (left) is presented at Court to Queen Elizabeth I (right) in 1593. (*Anthologia Hibernica*, Volume II)

Statue of Grace O'Malley at Westport House, Co. Mayo, Ireland. (Suzanne Mischyshyn / County Mayo – Westport House Grounds – Statue of Grace O'Malley (1530–1603) / CC BY-SA 2.0)

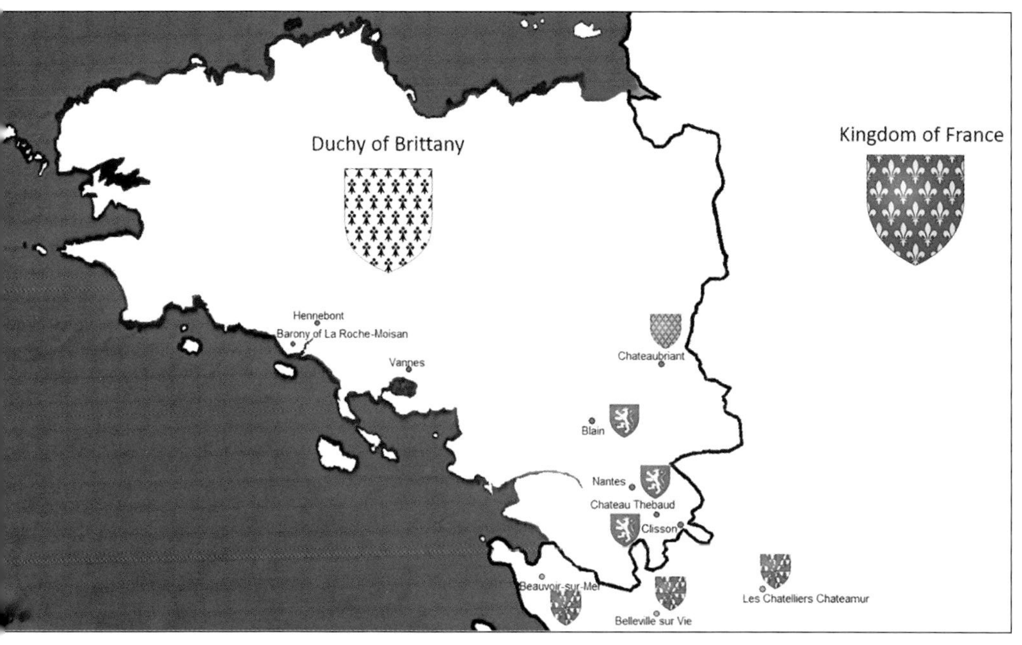

Map of the Clisson and Bellville estates in Brittany and France. (Caracal Rooikat, CC BY-SA 4.0)

Chateau de Clisson today. (Cyril5555, CC BY-SA 3.0)

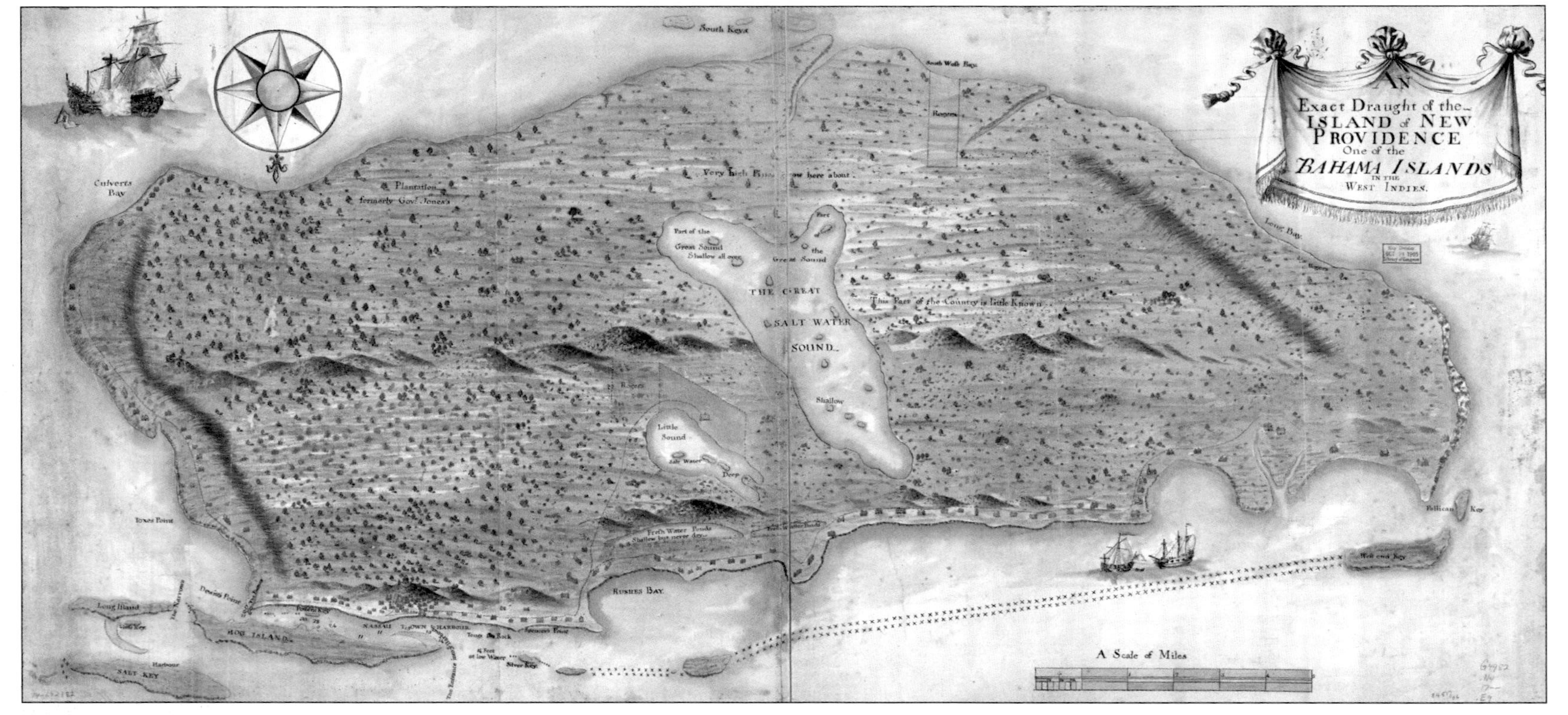

An exact draught of the island of New Providence one of the Bahama Islands in the West Indies. (Library of Congress, Geography and Map Division www.loc.gov/item/74692182/)

Port of Canton, 1800s. (Public domain)

Above: Pendennis Castle. (Public domain)

Left: Johann Schytte. (Finnish Heritage Agency, CC BY-SA 4.0)

Vowing revenge against the Crown, de Clisson sold her lands and then became the mistress of a series of noblemen, while raising the funds to buy and equip three warships. Between 1344 and 1357, she and her crews ruthlessly preyed upon French ships, murdering most of their crews, but always leaving a survivor to report her predations. Universally feared, after her near capture in 1357, de Clisson assumed a lower profile.

But her life as a pirate sailing the stormy seas bent on revenge and bloodthirsty murder did not begin that way. Jeanne-Louise de Belleville, de Clisson, Dame de Montaigu, was born in 1300 in Belleville-sur-Vie (Bellville on the River Vie) in the Vendée in the Gâtine Vendéenne along the French border with the Duchy of Brittany.

De Clisson was born into a noble family. Her father, Maurice IV, Montaigu of Belleville and Palluau (1263–1304), married her mother, Létice de Parthenay of Parthenay (1276–?). This was Maurice IV's second marriage as he had been previously wed to Sibille de Châteaubriant, who gave birth to a son, Maurice V, Montague of Belleville and Palluau (de Clisson's stepbrother). But Maurice V died in 1320, and because her father had no other male heirs, de Clisson stood to inherit her father's demesne, his seigneury – a titled lordship and lands.[1]

In the Bas-Poitou region, as a seigneur family the de Montaigu family probably had interests in local business, salt farming, winemaking and farming, and would be familiar with merchants and traders who travelled from rural to other markets as far as the Iberian Peninsula. This familiarity with trade would have included contacts with merchant shipping along the River Vie and along the coast of Poitou and Brittany with an island stronghold on Île d'Yeu initially settled by Irish monks, then sacked by Vikings. Île d'Yeu had impressive fortifications and several sheltered ports.[2]

We do not know much about de Clisson's childhood, other than tragedy struck her family when she was 4 years old and her father suddenly died. Scant records fail to reveal her mother remarrying.[3]

De Clisson was only 12 years old, in 1312, when she married a nobleman, 19-year-old Lord Geoffrey de Châteaubriant VIII (1293–1326),[4] a Breton nobleman. At the tender age of 19, Geoffrey de Châteaubriant VIII was already a widower, having previously been married to Alix de Thours.

De Clisson and Geoffrey de Châteaubriant VIII had two children, Geoffrey de Châteaubriant IX (1314–1347) and Louise de Châteaubriant (1316–1383).

But tragedy was to cast its dark shadow on their lives as de Clisson would outlive her son who died during the Battle of La Roche-Derrien during the Breton War of Succession (1341–1365).

Geoffrey de Châteaubriant IX died among the 4,000–5,000 French, Genoese and Breton soldiers fighting in the largest army ever to face the English on Breton soil, which was commanded by Charles de Blois, Duke of Brittany (reigned as duke from 1341 to 1364).[5]

After his death, his sister, Louise, inherited his lands and title as baroness. Louise married nobleman Guy de Laval XII.[6]

De Clisson was only 26 when her first husband died, leaving her with two children. Less than two years later, she married Guy de Penthièvre of the House of Penthièvre, widower of Joan de Avaugour (in France). Guy de Penthièvre was the second son of Charles de Blois, Duke of Brittany. It is possible de Clisson may have wanted to protect her underage children, by marrying. But the marriage was not a happy one, as de Penthièvre's family disliked her and objected to the marriage.

Members of the ducal family laid complaints with the bishops of Rennes and Vannes and to protect their family heritage an investigation was conducted on 10 February 1330. De Clisson's marriage was annulled by Pope John XX.[7] Guy de Penthièvre then married again, snagging the niece of King of France, Phillip IV (1268–1314), but his new marriage did not last long as he abruptly died the next year on 26 March 1331.

Jeanne de Belleville was attached to the Breviary of Belleville (1323–1326), a book of prayers that follow the liturgical year. This illustrated manuscript in French and Latin, is written in two volumes dated around 1323 to 1326 with illuminations by Jean Pucelle. De Clisson received it as a wedding gift when she married Olivier de Clisson IV. After her death, between 1379 and 1380, an inventory was made of King Charles V's property, and the breviary was identified as formerly belonging to de Clisson. Details of the Belleville Breviary of 1323 to 1326 are kept at the Bibliothèque Nationale, Paris (MS. Lat. 10484, folio 37 recto).

Undaunted and still marriageable, in 1330 de Clisson married Olivier de Clisson IV, a wealthy Breton who owned a manor house in Nantes, lands in Blain and an imposing castle at Clisson. This marriage was de Clisson IV's second and de Clisson's third. Olivier de Clisson IV was previously married to Blanche de Bonville (d.1329) and they had a son, Jean, who would in time inherit his mother's dower lands and become the Lord of Milly near Paris.

De Clisson, as the widow of the Geoffrey de Châteaubriant VIII, controlled areas in Poitou just south of the Breton border from Châteaumur in the south-east of Clisson to Beauvoir-sur-Mer in the west. In the marriage contract, there is evidence of de Clisson ensuring that the inheritances of her children from her previous marriage was legally secured. Combining these assets made de Clisson and de Clisson IV the seigneurial power[8] in the border region of Brittany. De Clisson and de Clisson IV eventually had five children: Isabeau (1325–1343), Maurice (1333–1334), Olivier V (1336–1407) – a future Constable of France also known as 'The Butcher' – Guillaume (1338–1345) – who died of exposure aged 7 – and Jeanne de Clisson Jr in 1340.

Sometime during their marriage, de Clisson was forced to take de Clisson IV to court to ensure her access to funds enumerated in their marriage contract. Astonishingly, King Philip VI (1293–1350) heard their case and ruled in her favour as there were witnesses who backed her up. The issues were resolved.[9]

But the Breton War of Succession was to be disastrous for de Clisson and de Clisson IV, as their families were divided on who to support, the English proponents for the duchy or the French. De Clisson and de Clisson IV supported Charles de Blois, while de Clisson IV's brothers did not. The French made Clisson castle their headquarters in 1342 as King Phillip VI sought to support Charles de Blois.

De Clisson IV was despatched as a commander to defend the city of Vannes, but after four failed attempts in 1342, the English finally captured the city and de Clisson IV too. Held as a noble hostage he was soon exchanged in a prisoner swap for the Ralph de Stafford, 1st Earl of Stafford. For his release a small sum was also asked for de Clisson IV, which made de Blois suspect De Clisson IV of failing to defend Vannes to the best of his ability. Such was de Blois's thinking when he accused de Clisson IV of treason.

The Truce of Malestroit was signed 13 January 1343 between France and England. Under perceived safe-conduct terms of truce, de Clisson IV and fifteen Breton lords were invited to a tournament where de Clisson IV was arrested and taken to Paris where he was tried.[10]

According to historian André Duchesne, writing 300 years later, the evidence against them was private correspondence between English King

Edward III (1312–1377) and the Breton lords trying to get them to change allegiance, which violated Section 9 of the Truce of Malestroit wherein no one in obedience of one king at the time of the signing, should put himself under obedience to the other for the duration of the treaty.

Desperate for her husband's life and her children's future, de Clisson tried to save him. Reportedly, she bribed a king's sergeant and was herself summoned before the Crown to answer charges of disobedience, rebellion and excesses against the king.[11]

Ever resourceful, de Clisson managed to evade arrest as her stepson, Jean de Clisson (now Lord of Milly) sheltered her at his castle about 55 kilometres east of Paris. Accompanied by Guilaume Bérard, Jean de Clisson's squire and valet, Guionnet de Fay and Guillaume Denart.[12]

Fearing the wrath of the Crown, Jean de Clisson himself took refuge in Brittany but abruptly died soon after. De Clisson ignored the summons and was found guilty in absentia in June 1343.[13, 14]

Unable to see his children and fearing for his wife's life, Olivier de Clisson IV, a brave knight, went to the scaffold and lost his head at Les Halles, the Paris marketplace, on 2 August 1343. From there, his corpse was drawn to the gibbet of Paris and there hung on the highest level, and his head was sent to Nantes in Brittany to be put on a lance over the city's Sauvetout Gate as a warning to others.[15] He died aged 43.

> In the year of our Grace one thousand three hundred and forty-three, on Saturday, the second day of August, Olivier, Lord of Clisson, knight, prisoner in the Chatelet of Paris for several treasons and other crimes perpetrated by him against the king and the crown of France, and for alliances that he made with the king of England, enemy of the king and kingdom of France, as the said Olivier ... has confessed, was by judgement of the king given at Orleans drawn from the Chatelet of Paris to Les Halles ... and there on a scaffold had his head cut off.[16]

De Clisson IV's grim execution shocked the landed nobility, as the evidence of his guilt had not been conclusive or publicly demonstrated and the execution process of desecrating and exposing a nobleman's body before all was primarily reserved for lower-class criminals. De Clisson IV's execution was judged harshly by Jean Froissart and his contemporaries.[17]

Fortune turned her back on de Clisson and her children as on 26 August 1343, for her attempted bribery of the king's sergeant, de Clisson was also charged with the crime of *lèse-majesté* (petty treason) and subsequently sentenced to banishment, with confiscation of her property.[18]

Gruesomely, de Clisson took her two young sons, Olivier V and Guillaume, from Clisson to Nantes, to show them their father's rotting head displayed at the Sauvetout Gate.

De Clisson, enraged by her husband's execution, swore retribution against King Philip VI and Charles de Blois. She considered their actions against her husband and family a cowardly murder.[19]

Before her property was seized she sold the de Clisson estates, raised a force of about 400 loyal men, and started attacking French forces in Brittany.[20] De Clisson reportedly attacked a castle at Touffou, near Bignon. The castle was built on the edge of a forest in the parish of Bignon, not far from the Abbey de Villeneuve, and was under command of Galois de la Heuse, an officer of Charles de Blois, Duke of Brittany, who, apparently, recognised de Clisson and let her in. Her forces followed her and massacred the entire garrison with the exception of one individual. She also razed a garrison at Château-Thébaud, about 20 kilometres south-east of Nantes, which had been a former post under the control of her late husband, Olivier de Clisson IV.

Flush with victories, de Clisson is believed to have converted three merchant ships for war, the beginning of her Black Fleet, so called as these vessels[21] may have also been painted black and their sails dyed red according to some references. Some versions of the story state that the English king and Breton sympathizers assisted her in this. Her flagship was, apparently, also named *My Revenge*.

The most common sailing ships available in Brittany at that time were flat-bottomed cargo ship with high sides and distinctive straight-angled stem and stern posts. The most visible giveaway that a ship was no longer just meant for cargo was if it had a forecastle or aftercastle constructed on it. Not all of these were permanent in structure and were not integrated into the hull.[22]

De Clisson's Black Fleet initially attacked shipping in the Bay of Biscay, probably from the aforementioned island fortress of Île d'Yeu, but eventually her fleet sailed into the English Channel hunting down French maritime merchant vessels. De Clisson was vicious and resolute. Her crews were instructed to kill all the men aboard the ships they took save one, who could tell the tale to the French king. This earned de Clisson the moniker, The Lioness of Brittany.[23]

Her commerce raiding is similar to guerrilla warfare. Its primary purpose is to disrupt the logistics of an enemy on the open seas by attacking merchant shipping rather than engaging actual military or naval combatants. A few ships would be used together as a swarming tactic. The crews would be equipped with grappling hooks and chains for boarding, and crossbows, swords and daggers.[24]

De Clisson is believed to have become trapped by the French at one point with her fleet while hiding at her Island fortress on Île d'Yeu. Locals told a story about the 'red men' (presumably English soldiers) who rescued her. Earlier in de Clisson's life, the lords of Belleville also owned the island. De Clisson had inherited Île d'Yeu from her deceased brother and had the old wooden fort demolished and replaced with a stone fortress. After she married Olivier de Clisson IV, he added to the design. This fortress was eventually one of her properties seized by the French Crown.[25]

While taking her revenge out on unsuspecting French sailors, in the 1350s, de Clisson married another military man, Walter Bentley,[26] one of English King Edward III's military deputies during the campaign. Bentley had been appointed King Edward III's lieutenant in Brittany in September 1350. In 1351, he lifted the sieges of Ploërmel and Fougeres and, on 4 August 1352, Bentley won the Battle of Mauron and was rewarded for his services with 'the lands and castles' of the island of Chauvet, Beauvoir-sur-Mer, Ampant, Barre, Blaye, Châteauneuf, Ville Maine, and the islands of Noirmoutier and Bouin.[27]

But their marriage would be plagued with ill-fortune, as disputes arose between the English lords taking lands in Brittany. As part of a treaty with Charles de Blois, Duke of Brittany, King Edward III ordered Bentley to surrender de Clisson's remaining castles in Brittany.[28]

Bentley refused and travelled to London to plead their cause. When he arrived, he was surprised to be imprisoned in the blood-soaked Tower of London while his case was heard. Eventually, he was released and allowed to return.[29]

However, worse was to come as the Black Death spread its infectious wings across Europe and the war ended as both nations were financially exhausted. The Black Death, which appeared in London in 1348, would within less than a decade killed between 30 and 50 per cent of Europe's population – about 25 million people or more.[30]

In January 1357, de Clisson and Bentley were granted the barony of La Roche-Moisan as compensation.[31] But their happily ever after did not last long, after de Clisson and Bentley finally settled at the Castle of Hennebont, a port town on the Brittany coast, which was in the territory of her allies, Bentley died in December 1359 and de Clisson a few weeks later, possibly of the pestilence sweeping Europe at the time, but we will never know for certain.

Appendix I

Further Points of Interest

The following is intended to give the reader a better understanding of the history of piracy, and what it was like during that time.

Women Pirates

Although it is usually assumed that pirates were men, during the Golden Age of Piracy, it is estimated that there were approximately forty women pirates.

What are pirates?

Maritime pirates are individuals who target ships for their cargo. They often use violence and do not follow international maritime laws.

What is the difference between pirates and buccaneers?

Pirates attack any ships regardless of nationality whereas buccaneers were a specific group of pirates operating in the Caribbean during the seventeenth and early-eighteenth centuries, who mainly targeted Spanish ships.

Who were privateers?

Privateers were individuals who were commissioned by governments to carry out private activities, including robbing merchant ships, but they were also authorised to hunt pirates. They were often ex-pirates themselves. In essence, they were pirates who were acting with the permission of the government.

What was the Brethen of the Coast?

The Brethen of the Coast was a coalition of pirates and buccaneers who were active in the seventeenth and early-eighteenth centuries, operating mainly off the coast of Tortuga Island and Port Royal in Jamaica.

What was the Golden Age of Piracy?

Between 1650–1720, ports in the Caribbean saw many pirates (French, Dutch and English mercenaries) operating as privateers under letters of Marque, enabling them to legitimately plunder ships of Spanish merchants, ostensibly to aid their sovereign's wars against Spain and her allies. Caribbean pirates repeatedly plundered Spanish ports all along the coast of South America and other Caribbean island ports held by the Spanish. Spanish treasure ships coming from Macao in the east were prime targets.

Origins of the Jolly Roger Flag

The Jolly Roger flag is a black flag with a white skull and crossbones. Its first use is believed to have been during the Golden Age of Piracy, possibly first used by pirate John 'Calico Jack' Rackham. Although used by many pirate ships, some would use a different flag or simply a black flag.

A Brief History of Hispañola

Christopher Columbus arrived on the island in 1492, naming it Hispañola. Many years later it was divided into two countries, modern-day Dominican Republic and Haiti.

What was the Holy Roman Empire?

The Holy Roman Empire was an alliance of various European countries, who supposedly held similar religious and political beliefs. It was headed by the Holy Roman Emperor who was elected by its members.

What was the Black Death?

Ancient Roman authors refer to plagues that swept the empire during the first through third centuries. They incorporated a goddess into their mythology specifically relating to epidemics of plague. The Roman plague that the celebrated physician Galen treated, and which decimated legions and killed co-emperor Lucius Verus, is believed today to have been smallpox.

Bubonic Plague, which swept Europe, first appeared as the Justinian Plague in 541–549. The Black Death occurred in 1346–1352 and wiped out almost 70 per cent of Europe's population. It devastated China as well. It is suspected today that the Black Death plague may have originated in Mongolia among marmots and was transferred through infected marmot-skin pelts to Venice and Europe.

Kings and Queens of England

Many women pirates were often brought to the attention of the English monarchy. Some even had dealings with the monarch themselves.

King Edward III (r.1327–1377)
King George I (r.1714–1727)
King Henry VIII (r.1509–1547)
King James I (r.1603–1625) (also known as King James VI of Scotland) (r.1567–1603 (when the English and Scottish realm was united until his death in 1625))
Queen Elizabeth I (r.1558–1603)
Queen Mary I (r.1553–1558)

Kings of France

King Charles VIII (r.1483–1498)
King Francis I (r.1515–1547)
King Henry II (r.1547–1559)
King Louis XIV (r.1643–1715)
King Phillip IV (r.1285–1314)
King Philip VI (r.1328–1350)

Appendix II

Interesting Facts About Pirates

How far do pirates date back?

As far back as the Achaemenid Empire (founded 550 BCE), predating Greek and Roman civilizations.

Were all pirates outcasts?

This is a myth, not all pirates were outcasts. Many men (and women) simply turned to piracy because of their difficult circumstances.

Did pirates really bury their treasure?

There are many stereotypes associated with pirates, one being that they buried their loot or treasure. This is not true, and, in fact, pirates would often spend their gains quickly.

What valuable goods did pirates hope to acquire?

Despite the stereotype that pirates were looking for gold and jewels, they often looted alcohol, food, spices and textiles.

Did pirates really wear eye patches?

Yes, pirates did tend to wear eye patches as eye injuries were common to a life of fighting.

What did pirates eat?

Pirates (as with many sailors) suffered from poor diets and would often get scurvy due to a lack of Vitamin C. Hence why, in later years, pirates and sailors would take limes on long trips. Food would rot quickly at sea so pirates (and sailors) would rely on cured meats and fermented (pickled) vegetables, which would keep longer. They may also have taken live animals on board to use as a source of milk and eggs, and eventually fresh meat. They carried stores of dried vegetables, beans, peas, etc. They also ate fish, porpoises, seals and other marine animals. In the Caribbean they smoked and cured wild cattle and pigs.

What was the life expectancy of a pirate?

Although this varied, so it is difficult to speculate what the average life expectancy of a pirate was, many men (or women) would usually have been in their twenties or thirties when at sea. Due to a poor diet, as well as illnesses and hard work, this meant that many pirates had a short life expectancy. Many executed pirates were in their 20s. A few celebrated captains lived to retire after taking the King's pardon. On average, life at sea was rigorous and dangerous and most pirates whose histories have come down to us were in their 20s and 30s.

Were pirates democratic?

Yes, those among the Brethren of the Coast had a set of strict rules governing behaviour aboard ship and divisions of spoils. They voted for captains and on which ports to plunder or prizes to take. They had a level of democratic equivalency among their crews unknown in British or Colonial Navies. They also freed slaves if they would join them.

Did pirates follow codes of conduct?

Yes, pirates generally abided by rules and the ship's code of conduct.

Do pirates still exist?

Although less common in the modern age, pirates do still exist, although they use modern tactics and weapons.

Were all pirates men?

This book has proven that this is the biggest myth of all, not all pirates were (or are) men!

Appendix III

Other Women Pirates

Although the most famous women pirates have been discussed throughout this book, there were many more well-known women pirates who operated the seas, some of whom are listed below:

Hung Bamei
Also known as: **Hung P'ei-mei or Hung P'emel**
Date of birth: **1906**
Place of birth: **Jinshan District, Shanghai, China**
Date of death: **4 May 1982**
Place of death: **Taipei City, Taiwan**
A Chinese pirate who served as a naval commander in the Sino-Japanese War (1937–1945). She also served during the Chinese Civil War (1945–1949).

Mrs Beare
Full name: **Unknown**
Also known as: **Mrs Bear**
Date of birth: **Seventeenth century?**
Place of birth: **Jamaica**
Married: **Captain John Phillip Beare (also known as Captain John Phillip Bear)**
Date of death: **Seventeenth century?**
Place of death: **Jamaica**
Her full name is unknown, she was married to her pirate husband, Captain John Phillip Beare (whose surname was also spelt Bear). It is believed that she originated from Jamaica and often worn men's clothes when aboard ships. Operating as a pirate together with her husband in the Caribbean during the seventeenth century.

Flora Burn
Date of birth: Eighteenth century?
Place of birth: United States of America
Date of death: Eighteenth century?
Place of death: Unknown
Ship: HMS *Revenge*
Burn served aboard the privateer ship HMS *Revenge* as a sailor. It is believe that she operated in North American waters.

Mary Critchett
Also known as: Mary Crichett
Mary Crickett
Date of birth: Early seventeenth century
Date of birth: England?
Date of death: 1729
Place of death: Viriginia, United States of America
Critchett was tried for piracy in Virginia in the United States of America, together with five male crewmen, all of whom were executed.

Elise Eskilsdotter
Also known as: Elise Nilsson
Date of birth: ?
Place of birth: Norway
Married: Olav Nilsson
Date of death: *c.*1483
Place of death: Norway
A Norwegian pirate who operated during the fifteenth century. She originated from the Norwegian nobility. The daughter of knight Eskild Ågesen and Elisbeth Jakobsdatter Hegle, she married nobleman Olav Nilsson (*c.*1400–1455) in *c.*1420 and they had children together. Nilsson was assassinated and following his death, she sought revenge against his murders.

Martha Farley
Date of birth: Early eighteenth century?
Place of birth: England?
Date of death: 1726
Place of death: Virginia, United States of America

Farley was caught and tried for piracy in Virginia in the United States of America. She was tried along side three men. All the men were executed for their crime, but Farley was spared by the court.

Ingela Gathenhielm
Date of birth: 1692
Place of birth: Sweden
Married: Lars Gathenhielm (also known as Lars Andersson Gathe)
Date of death: 1729
Place of death: Sweden

A Swedish pirate who married pirate Lars Gathenhielm (also known as Lars Andersson Gathe (1689–1718). She took over her husband's pirate business upon his death.

Martha Herring
Also known as: Martha Gordon
Date of birth: 1714
Place of birth: England
Married: Sandy Gordon
Date of death: 1735
Place of death: Unknown
Ship: ***Flying Scot***

It is understood that Herring's father was killed in a mutiny by her then lover Sandy Gordon, whom she later married, but he died shortly thereafter in 1715. It is believed that Herring and Gordon were pirates aboard the ship, *Flying Scot*.

Maria Lindsey

Also known as: Maria Cobham
Date of birth: Eighteenth century?
Place of birth: England
Date of death: Eighteenth century?
Place of death: Unknown

Believed to have been a sex worker who married pirate Eric Cobham (*c*.1700–1760). It is understood that she may have had mental health issues. Lindsey operated as a pirate in the seas off New England and Newfoundland, near Canada.

Elizabetha Patrickson

Date of birth: Seventeenth century?
Place of birth: Unknown
Married: William Patrickson
Date of death: Seventeenth century?
Place of death: Unknown

She raided English ships together with her husband, William Patrickson. Eventually, she was caught and tried in an English court where she was tortured until she confessed and was later hanged.

Rachel Wall

Date of birth: *c*.1760
Place of birth: United States of America?
Date of death: 1789
Place of death: Unknown

One of the most famous American women pirates. She operated as a pirate together with her husband during the eighteenth century. Wall is believed to be the first American woman pirate.

Notes

Links that my be lost over time may yet be found by accessing the Internet's Wayback Machine at archive.org:
https://help.archive.org/help/using-the-wayback-machine

Chapter 1: Anne Bonny and The Republic of Pirates

1. Johnson, Captain Charles (also known as Defoe, Daniel), *A General History of the Robberies and Murders of the Most Notorious Pyrates*,1724, p.16
2. Johnson, Captain Charles (also known as Defoe, Daniel), *A General History of the Robberies and Murders of the Most Notorious Pyrates*,1724, p.19
3. Wise Money Rum, https://wisemonkeyrum.com/blog/rum-and-gunpowder-the-cocktail-favoured-by-the-bold
4. Jamaica National Archives, *The Tryals of Captain John Rackham and Others*, 1721, p.11
5. Ibid
6. Ibid
7. Collins, Dr A.R., *British Cannon Design (1600–1800*), Miscellany, https://www.arc.id.au
8. James Ford Bell Library, online exhibitions and instructional resources, *Anne Bonny Early Life*, https://gallery.lib.umn.edu/exhibits/show/mary-read-anne-bonny/anne-bonny/anne-bonny--early life
9. Jamaica National Archives, *The Tryals of Captain John Rackham and Others*, 1721, p.11
10. Jamaica National Archives, *The Tryals of Captain John Rackham and Others*, 1721, p.12
11. Ibid
12. Jamaica National Archives, *The Tryals of Captain John Rackham and Others*, 1721, p.18
13. Jamaica National Archives, *The Tryals of Captain John Rackham and Others*, 1721, p.19
14. Ibid
15. Ibid
16. *Annals of Kinsale: The Council Book of the Corporation of Kinsale, From 1652 to 1800*, p.lxiii
17. James Ford Bell Library, online exhibitions and instructional resources, *Anne Bonny Early Life*, https://gallery.lib.umn.edu/exhibits/show/mary-read-anne-bonny/anne-bonny/anne-bonny--early life
18. *Annals of Kinsale: The Council Book of the Corporation of Kinsale, From 1652 to 1800*, p.lxiiv

19. *Annals of Kinsale: The Council Book of the Corporation of Kinsale, From 1652 to 1800*, p.lxxix
20. *Annals of Kinsale: The Council Book of the Corporation of Kinsale, From 1652 to 1800*, p.lxiv
21. Munro, Sophie, *Anne Bonny 1690–1778*, 2 March 2017, Women's History Network, https://womenshistorynetwork.org/anne-bonny-c-1690-c-1778
22. Wikipedia, https://en.wikipedia.org/wiki/South_Sea_Company
23. Stewart, Terry, *The South Seas Bubble*, Historic UK, https://www.historicuk.com/HistoryUK/HistoryofEngland/South-Sea-Bubble
24. Johnson, Captain Charles (also known as Defoe, Daniel), *A General History of the Robberies and Murders of the Most Notorious Pyrates*, 1724, p.132
25. James Ford Bell Library, online exhibitions and instructional resources, *Anne Bonny Early Life*, https://gallery.lib.umn.edu/exhibits/show/mary-read-anne-bonny/anne-bonny/anne-bonny--early life
26. Johnson, Captain Charles (also known as Defoe, Daniel), *A General History of the Robberies and Murders of the Most Notorious Pyrates*, 1724, p.132
27. Ibid
28. Cawthorne, Nigel, *A History of Pirates, Blood and Thunder on the High Seas*, Capella, United States of America, 2003, p.208
29. Ibid
30. Woodard, Colin, *The Republic of Pirates Being the True and Surprising Story of the Caribbean Pirates and The Man Who Brought Them Down*, Harcourt, United States of America, 2007, p.316
31. Ibid
32. Woodard, Colin, *The Republic of Pirates Being the True and Surprising Story of the Caribbean Pirates and The Man Who Brought Them Down*, Harcourt, United States of America, 2007
33. Johnson, Captain Charles (also known as Defoe, Daniel), *A General History of the Pyrates*,1724
34. Woodard, Colin, *The Republic of Pirates Being the True and Surprising Story of the Caribbean Pirates and The Man Who Brought Them Down*, Harcourt, United States, 2007, p.317
35. Cawthorne, Nigel, *A History of Pirates, Blood and Thunder on the High Seas*, Capella, United States of America, 2003, p.308
36. Woodard, Colin, *The Republic of Pirates Being the True and Surprising Story of the Caribbean Pirates and The Man Who Brought Them Down*, Harcourt, United States, 2007, p.317
37. Woodard, Colin, *The Republic of Pirates Being the True and Surprising Story of the Caribbean Pirates and The Man Who Brought Them Down*, Harcourt, United States of America, 2007, p.318
38. Woodard, Colin, *The Republic of Pirates Being the True and Surprising Story of the Caribbean Pirates and The Man Who Brought Them Down*, Harcourt, United States, 2007, p.319

39. Cawthorne, Nigel, *A History of Pirates, Blood and Thunder on the High Seas*, Capella, United States of America, 2003, p.25
40. Munro, Sophie, *Anne Bonny 1690–1778*, 2 March 2017, Women's History Network, https://womenshistorynetwork.org/anne-bonny-c-1690-c-1778

Chapter 2: Mary Read, Three's Company

1. Cawthorne, Nigel, *A History of Pirates, Blood and Thunder on the High Seas*, Capella, United States of America, 2003 p.208
2. Cordingly, David, *Seafaring Women: Adventures of Pirate Queens, Female Stowaways, and Sailors' Wives*, Random House, Trade paperback edition, New York, 2007
3. Woodard, Colin, *The Republic of Pirates Being the True and Surprising Story of the Caribbean Pirates and The Man Who Brought Them Down*, Harcourt, United States of America, 2007, p.317

Chapter 3: Marie-Anne Dieu-le-Veut, God Willing

1. Ryzhov, Valery, *Filibusters and Corsairs*, 'Top War' article, 30 July 2018, p.1
2. Library of Congress Global Gateway, *King's Daughters, Casket Girls, Prostitutes*
3. Bone, Katherine, *The History of Maritime Piracy Pirates and Privateers*, Pirates and Privateers, The History of Maritime Piracy (Cindy Vallar, Editor and Reviewer), http//www.cindyvallar.com/Tortuga.html
4. Bone, Katherine, *The History of Maritime Piracy Pirates and Privateers*, Pirates and Privateers, The History of Maritime Piracy (Cindy Vallar, Editor and Reviewer), http//www.cindyvallar.com/Tortuga.html, p.2
5. Cawthorne, Nigel, *A History of Pirates: Blood and Thunder on the High Seas*, Arcturus Publishing, London, 2003, p.55, reference from Alexander Exquemelin, former buccaneer surgeon, in his book *De Americanensche Zee-Roovers* (American Sea Rovers also known as Buccaneers of America), Amsterdam, 1678, Library of Congress, https://www.loc.gov/exhibits/exploring-the-early-americas/interactives/buccaneers-of-america/
6. Wagner, B.B., *Be My Matelotage! The Civil Union of 17th Century Pirates*, 2006, Ancient Origins, https://www.ancient-origins.net/history-ancient-traditions/matelotage-0012504
7. Burg, B.R., *Sodomy and the Pirate Tradition: English Sea Rovers in the Seventeenth-Century Caribbean*, second edition, New York, University Press, New York, United States of America, 2005, p.260
8. Thornbury, Walter, *Monarchs of the Main*, London, 1861, Chapter 1, p.B2., US Archives, https://ia904607.us.archive.org/17/items/monarchsofmain00thorrich/monarchsofmain00thorrich.pdf
9. Bruyneel, Mark, *A Short History of Tortuga, 1625–1688*, Isle of Tortuga, Zeerovery, http://zeerovery.nl/history/tortuga.html
10. Milligan, Mark, author *Heritage Daily*, *Tortuga: The Pirate Stronghold*, 30 December 2020, *Heritage Daily*, https://www.heritagedaily.com/2020/12/tortuga-the-pirate-stronghold/136613

11. Cawthorne, Nigel, *A History of Pirates: Blood and Thunder on the High Seas*, Arcturus Publishing, London, 2003, p.63
12. Margry, Pierre, *Relations et Mémoires Inédits pour Servir à L'histoire de la France sous les Pays D'outre-mer Tirés des Archives du Ministère de la Marine et des Colonies, Challamel*, 1867
13. Seymour, *Jean-Jacques, Les Chemins des Proies: une Histoire de la Flibuste, Ibis Rouge Éd.*, 2010, p.299

Chapter 4: Neel Cupyer and The Perils of the Great Pox

1. Thornbury, Walter, *Monarchs of the Main,* 1861, Preface iii
2. Captivating History, *The Golden Age of Piracy: A Captivating History to the Role of Pirates in Maritime History During the Early Modern Period, Including Stories of Anne Bonny, Sir Francis Drake And William Kidd (Early Modern History)*, Captivating History, 2021, p.100
3. Zuidhoek, Arne, *Heet Nel Cuyper: Avonturierster van Oudewater; een biografie (Lady Pirates)*, Utrecht, 2019
4. Ibid
5. Frith, John, *Syphilis: Its Early History and Treatment Until Penicillin and the Debate on its Origins*, JVMH Volume 20, Number 4, Journal of Military and Veterans History
6. Ibid

Chapter 5: Jacquotte Delahaye, Real or Phantom?

1. Breverton, Terry, *A Gross of Pirates From Alfhild the Shield Maiden to Afweyne the Big Mouth,* Amberley Publishing, Stroud, 2018
2. *The Legend of Jacquotte Delahaye*, The LeEms Machine, https://theleemsmachine.com/bean/blog/2022/01/12/the-legend-of-jacquotte-delahaye/
3. Ibid
4. Owen, Erika, Wright, Alexander (Illustrator), *Lawbreaking Ladies: 50 Tales of Daring, Defiant, and Dangerous Women from History*, S&S/Simon Element, United States of America, 23 March 2021, pp.6–7
5. Duncombe, Laura Snook, *Pirate Women: The Princesses, Prostitutes, and Privateers Who Ruled the Seven Seas*, Chicago Review Press, Chicago, United States of America, 2017
6. Bruyneel, Mark, *A Short History of Tortuga, 1625–1688*, Isle of Tortuga, http://zeerovery.nl/history/tortuga.html
7. Ibid
8. Ibid
9. Owen, Erika, Wright, Alexander (Illustrator), *Lawbreaking Ladies: 50 Tales of Daring, Defiant, and Dangerous Women from History*, S&S/Simon Element, United States of America, 23 March 2021, pp.6–7, 177
10. Parker, Charles H., *Global Interactions in the Early Modern Age, 1400–1800*, Cambridge University Press, Cambridge, 2010

Chapter 6: Gráinne O'Malley, Pirate Queen of Connacht

1. Murray, Theresa D., 'Early Modern History (1500–1700)', Issue 2, Volume 13, March–April 2005
2. Graunille: Grace O'Malley – Ireland's Pirate Queen, 2011, Grace O'Malley, Anne Chambers, https://www.graceomalley-annechambers.com
3. Ibid
4. Ibid
5. *Gaeltacht The Living Communities*, Gaelta, https://gaelta.ie/Gráinne-omalley-the-pirate-queen
6. *Exploring Celtic Civilizations*, Exploring Celtic Civilizations, https://exploringcelticciv.web.unc.edu/1537-act-for-the-english-order-habit-and-language
7. Smith, Emily, *Never the Twain Shall Part: A Comparison and Analysis of Irish and English Marriage Laws Following the English Conquest of Ireland*, Masters Thesis, 2010, p.18
8. Share Ok, https://shareok.org/bitstream/handle/11244/9085/Smith_okstate_0664M_10808.pdf?sequence=1&isAllowed=y
9. Cambridge University Press, *Dictionary of Irish Biography*, Cambridge University Press, Cambridge, 2010, https://dib.cambridge.org
10. Ibid
11. Ibid
12. Gráinne O'Malley, https://www.dib.ie/biography/omalley-Gráinne-grace-granuaile-a6886

Chapter 7: Sayyida al-Hurra, Queen of the Barbary Pirates

1. *Daily Mail*, https://www.dailymail.co.uk/news/article-13708787/Controversial-treasure-hunters-discovered-pirate-shipwreck.html
2. Memissi, Fatima, *The Forgotten Queens of Islam*, University of Minnesota Press, Minnesota, United States of America, 1997, p.115
3. Verde, Tom, *Malika* (Queen), January/February 2017 and Special Edition, 2021, AramcoWorld, https://www.aramcoworld.com/Articles/January-2017/Malika-VI-Sayyida-Al-Hurra
4. Grimau, Rodolfo Gil (Benumeya), '*Sayyida al-Hurra, Mujer Marroquí de Origen Andalusí*', *Anaquel de Estudios Árabes*, 11:311, January 2000
5. Verde, Tom, *Malika* (Queen), January/February 2017 and Special Edition, 2021, AramcoWorld, https://www.aramcoworld.com/Articles/January-2017/Malika-VI-Sayyida-Al-Hurra
6. Ibid
7. Ibid
8. Memissi, Fatima, *The Forgotten Queens of Islam*, University of Minnesota Press, Minnesota, United States of America, 1997, p.118
9. Verde, Tom, *Malika* (Queen), January/February 2017 and Special Edition, 2021, AramcoWorld, https://www.aramcoworld.com/Articles/January-2017/Malika-VI-Sayyida-Al-Hurra

Chapter 8: Zhèng Shí, From Flower Boats to the Red Flag Fleet

1. Cordingly, David, *Pirates: An Illustrated History of Privateers, Buccaneers & Pirates from the Sixteenth Century to the Present, Salamander Books Limited, London, 1996, p.230. The book notes mention that 'this fanciful depiction is from History of Pirates of All Nations published in 1836'.*
2. Murray, Dian H., Pirates of the South China Coast, 1790–1810, Stanford University Press, Stanford, California, United States of America, 1987, pp.71, 143
3. Cole, Bernard D., *The Great Wall at Sea: China's Navy in the Twenty-First Century*, Naval Institute Press, Annapolis, United States of America, 2010, p.xvi
4. *Ye, Lingfeng,* 张保仔的传说和真相, *The Myths and Truths of Zhang Bao the Kid, Nanchang, Jiangx,* 江西教育出版社, *2012*
5. Wikipedia, https://en.wikipedia.org/wiki/Zheng_Yi_Sao#CITEREFYe2012
6. Po, Chung-yam, Heidelberg University, https://archiv.ub.uni-heidelberg.de/volltextserver/18877/1/PhD_Dissertation_CyPO.pdf, *Conceptualizing the Blue Frontier*, p.66
7. Andrew, Elizabeth Wheeler and Bushnell, Katharine Caroline, *Heathen Slaves and Christian Rulers, Echo Library, Echo Library, 2006, p.11*
8. Andrew, Elizabeth Wheeler and Bushnell, Katharine Caroline, *Heathen Slaves and Christian Rulers, Echo Library*, Echo Library, 2006, p.12
9. *The Great Qing and the Maritime World in the Long Eighteenth Century*
10. Yvan, Melchoir, *Inside Canton*, Henry Vizetelly, Gough Square, London, 1858, Chapter 9
11. The Canton System, Wikipedia, https://en.wikipedia.org/wiki/Canton_System
12. Murray, Dian H., Pirates of the South China Coast, 1790–1810, Stanford University Press, Stanford, California, United States of America, 1987, p.64
13. Wikipedia, https://en.wikipedia.org/wiki/Zheng_Yi_(pirate)
14. Wikipedia, https://en.wikipedia.org/wiki/Zheng_Yi_Sao
15. Ibid
16. Ibid
17. Neumann, Charles Fried, *The History of Pirates Who Infested the China Sea: From 1807 to 1810*, Fb&c Limited, 2017
18. Cunliffe, Ciaran, *Cheung Po Tsai and Ching Shih: Pirate Monarchs*, Head Stuff, https://headstuff.org/culture/history/ching-shih-and-cheung-po-tsai-pirate-monarchs/
19. Ibid
20. Ibid
21. Smith, Amy, *Meet Ching Shih: The Prostitute-Turned-Pirate Who Banned Rape in Her 50,000-Man Fleet*, 25 July 2018, New Historian, https://www.newhistorian.com/wp-content/uploads/2018/07/Ching-Shih-1-1.jpg
22. *The Battle of Tiger Mouth*, Wikipedia, https://en.wikipedia.org/wiki/Battle_of_the_Tiger%27s_Mouth

23. Alvarez, Jorge, *The Chinese Woman Who Became Queen of Piracy with a Fleet of Hundreds of Ships, LBV Independent Magazine of Culture, 2020*
24. Banerji, Urvija, *Ching Shih, Who Lived and Pillaged During the Qing Dynasty, Has Been Called the Most Successful Pirate in History, Atlas Obscura, https://www.atlasobscura.com/articles/ching-shih-chinese-female-pirate*

Chapter 9: Queen Teuta of the Ardiaei

1. Wilkes, John, *The Illyrians*, Wiley-Blackwell, United States of America, 1992, p.160
2. Polybius and Shuckburgh, E. (translator), *Histories*, Book 2, Number 5, MacMillan, London, 1889
3. Wilkes, John, *The Illyrians*, Wiley-Blackwell, United States of America, 1992, p.160
4. Wilkes, John, *The Illyrians*, Wiley-Blackwell, United States of America, 1992, p.159
5. Parkinson, William A. (editor), *The Archaeology of Tribal Societies*, 'Modeling [*sic*] the Evolution and Formation of an Illyrian Tribal System' by Galaty, Michael L., Berghahn Books, New York, United States of America, 2002 Chapter 7, p.113
6. Boardman, John, Edwards, I.E.S., Hammond; N.G.L. and Sollberger, E. (eds.), *The Cambridge Ancient History: The Prehistory of the Balkans, the Middle East and the Aegean World, Tenth to Eighth Centuries BC*, Volume III, Part 1, Second Edition, Cambridge University Press, Cambridge, 1982
7. Altuntaş, Leman, *Queen of the Seas who Challenged Rome: 'Queen Teuta'*, Arkeonews, 31 October 2023
8. Kretschmer, P., *Einleitung in die Geschichte der Griechischen Sprachen*, Göttingen, 1896
9. Strabo, *Geographica*, Volume I, 7 BCE (last printed during his lifetime in 23 CE)
10. Polybius and Shuckburgh, E. (translator), *Histories*, Book 2, Number 9, MacMillan, London, 1889
11. Strabo, *Geographica*, Volume I, 7 BCE (last printed during his lifetime in 23 CE), Books 1 and 2, Chapter 7
12. Strabo, *Geographica*, Volume I, 7 BCE (last printed during his lifetime in 23 CE)
13. Polybius and Shuckburgh, E. (translator), *Histories*, Book 2, Number 9, MacMillian, London, 1889
14. Strabo, *Geographica*, Volume I, 7 BCE (last printed during his lifetime in 23 CE), Books 1 and 2, Chapter 7
15. Polybius and Shuckburgh, E. (translator), *Histories*, Book 2, Number 11, MacMillan, London, 1889
16. Polybius and Shuckburgh, E. (translator), *Histories*, Book 2, Number 12, MacMillan, London, 1889
17. Altuntaş, Leman, *Queen of the Seas who Challenged Rome: 'Queen Teuta'*, Arkeonews, 31 October 2023

Chapter 10: Lady Elizabeth Killigrew, All in the Family

1. Geni, https://www.geni.com/people/Lady-Elizabeth Killigrew/6000000001531288646
2. Geni, https://www.geni.com/people/Capt-John Killigrew/6000000001531288654

3. https://commons.wikimedia.org/wiki/File:Pendennis_Castle.jpg
4. Ibid
5. Wikipedia, https://en.wikipedia.org/wiki/Device_Forts
6. Ibid
7. History of Parliament, https://www.historyofparliamentonline.org/volume/1558-1603/member/killigrew-john-i-1584
8. Cornish Bird Blog, https://cornishbirdblog.com/the-notorious-women-of-the-killigrew-family/
9. Ibid
10. Ibid
11. Ibid
12. Wikipedia, https://en.wikipedia.org/wiki/Mary_Wolverston
13. History of Parliament, https://www.historyofparliamentonline.org/volume/1558-1603/member/killigrew-john-i-1584
14. Ibid
15. Ibid
16. Ibid
17. Ibid
18. Wikipedia, https://en.wikipedia.org/wiki/Mary_Wolverston#cite_note-AWS-8
19. Emerson Kathy Lynn, *A Who's Who of Tudor Women*, Kathy Lynn Emerson, 2020
20. Sharp, Anne Wallace, *Daring Pirate Women*, Lerner Publications, United States of America, 2002, pp.45–46

Chapter 11: Christina Anna Skytte, Brothers, Sisters and Lovers

1. Sylvander, Gustaf Volmar, *Kalmar stads och slotts historia*, Sweden, 1865
2. 'Anna Christina Skytte', Sörmlands Museum. Archived from the original on 2 April 2015
3. Adelsvapen, https://www.adelsvapen.com/genealogi/Skytte_af_Duderhof_nr_8
4. Ibid
5. Ibid
6. Ibid
7. Ibid
8. Elgenstierna, G. and Ättartavlor, Svenska Adelns, *Index to Muster Rolls*, Volume 7, Swedish Krigsarkiv, Stockholm, Sweden, 1864, pp.319–320 and Kvinnor, Svenska Män och, *Anteckningar om Svenska Qvinnor*, Volume 7, Stockholm, Sweden,1864, pp.94, 341
9. Wikipedia, https://en.wikipedia.org/wiki/Maria_Skytte and University of St Andrew's, https://www.st-andrews.ac.uk/history/ssne/item.php?id=4921
10. de Palafox y Mendoza, Juan, *Dialogo político del estado de Alemania y comparación de España con las demás naciones*, More Than Books, 'Clasicos Hispánicos', Madrid, Spain, 2015 and de Palafox y Mendoza, Juan, *Diálogo político del estado de Alemania*, Spain, 1632?
11. Swartz, Stuart B., *Copper Dreams and the 'Hope of the North': Sweden, Portugal and Spain During the Portuguese Rebellion (1640–1668)*, Part I, p.28

12. Swartz, Stuart B., *Copper Dreams and the 'Hope of the North.' Sweden, Portugal and Spain During the Portuguese Rebellion, 1640–1668,* Part I, Politika, p. 28
13. Ibid
14. Swartz, Stuart B., *Copper Dreams and the 'Hope of the North.' Sweden, Portugal and Spain During the Portuguese Rebellion, 1640–1668,* Part I, Politika, p.29
15. Wikipedia, https://en.wikipedia.org/wiki/Dano-Swedish_War_(1657%E2%80%931658)
16. Ibid
17. Murdoch, Steve and Grosjean, Alexia, University of St Andrews, Institute of Scottish Historical Research SKYTTE, GUSTAV ADOLF (SSNE 4921), University of St Andrews, https://www.st-andrews.ac.uk/history/ssne/item.php?id=4921
18. Murdoch, Steve and Grosjean, Alexia, University of St Andrews, Institute of Scottish Historical Research HAMILTON, BRITA MARGARETHA (SSNE 6386), University of St Andrews, https://www.st-andrews.ac.uk/history/ssne/item.php?id=6386
19. Murdoch, Steve and Grosjean, Alexia, University of St Andrews, Institute of Scottish Historical Research, HAMILTON, HUGH (SSNE 2582), University of St Andrews, https://www.st-andrews.ac.uk/history/ssne/item.php?id=2582
20. Murdoch, Steve and Grosjean, Alexia, University of St Andrews, Institute of Scottish Historical Research, FORRAT, MARGAREHTA (SSNE 6267), University of St Andrews, https://www.st-andrews.ac.uk/history/ssne/item.php?id=6267
21. Rikarkivet (in Swedish/translated from Swedish Gustaf Drake Biografi), https://sok.riksarkivet.se/sbl/Presentation.aspx?id=17630
22. Ibid
23. Ibid
24. Ibid
25. Fryxell, Anders, *Berättelser ur svenska historien*, Sweden, 1846
26. Rikarkivet (in Swedish/translated from Swedish Gustaf Drake Biografi), https://sok.riksarkivet.se/sbl/Presentation.aspx?id=17630
27. Amirell, Stefan Eklöf, 'Christina Anna Skytte', (article by Amirell, Stefan Eklöf) retrieved 27 August 2024, Svenskt kvinnobiografiskt lexikon, https://www.skbl.se/sv/artikel/AnnaSkytte
28. Rikarkivet (in Swedish/translated from Swedish Gustaf Drake Biografi), https://sok.riksarkivet.se/sbl/Presentation.aspx?id=17630
29. Ibid
30. Murdoch, Steve and Grosjean, Alexia, University of St Andrews, Institute of Scottish Historical Research, SKYTTE, GUSTAV ADOLF (SSNE 4921), University of St Andrews, https://www.st-andrews.ac.uk/history/ssne/item.php?id=4921https://www.standrews.ac.uk/history/ssne/item.php?id=4921
31. Amirell, Stefan Eklöf, 'Christina Anna Skytte', (article by Amirell, Stefan Eklöf) retrieved 27 August 2024, Svenskt kvinnobiografiskt lexikon, https://www.skbl.se/sv/artikel/AnnaSkytte

Chapter 12: Jeanne de Clisson, The Lioness of Brittany

1. Vendeens Archives, http://vendeens-archives.vendee.fr
2. Heebøll-Holm, Thomas, K. *Ports, Piracy and Maritime War: Piracy in the English Channel and the Atlantic,* c.*1280*–c.*1330 (Medieval Law and Its Practice)*, Brill, Netherlands, 2013
3. Hajdu, R. 'Family and Feudal Ties in Poitou, 1100–1300', *The Journal of Interdisciplinary History*, Volume 8, Number 1, summer 1977, pp.117–139 (twenty-three pages), Sumption, Jonathan, *The Hundred Years' War*, The MIT Press, Massachusetts, United States of America, p.55 and Goude, Charles, *Histoire de Châteaubriant. Baronnie, Ville et Paroisse*, Oberthur et fils Rennes, France, 1870 p.33
4. Geni, https://www.geni.com/people/Geoffroy-VIII-de-Ch%C3%A2teaubriant/6000000013087519492
5. Sumption, Jonathan, *The Hundred Years' War: Trial by Battle*, Volume 1, Faber and Faber, London, 1990
6. Buffé, Marcel, *Châteaubriant, une cité dans l'histoire: De la préhistoire à nos jours*, Éditions Cid, 1983, p.15.
7. Note: On 10 February 1330, in Avignon, France, at the request of Guy de Bretagne, Pope Jean XXII appointed the bishops of Rennes and Vannes to investigate the alleged marriage that was supposedly contracted in 1328 by Jeanne de Belleville, widow of the Lord of Chateaubriant, and Guy de Bretagne, seigneur de Penthievre. Mollat, G., op cit, pj, Number II pp.49–50. See also Jean XXII (1316–1334) *Lettres Secretes et Curiales* relating to France, by Coulon, A. and Clemencet, S. If Jeanne could not deny Guy's words. Guy could remarry. Mollat, G. op cit, p.47. A little later, on 30 April 1330, Jeanne de Belleville, widow of Geoffroy de Chateaubriant, asked the Holy See for a dispensation to marry Olivier de Clisson. Mollat, G. op cit, p.47, after Vatican Register, Number 95, Lettres commune 81. See John XXII (1316–1334). Joint letters analysed according to the so-called Avignon or Vatican registers by Mollat, G. (1921–1947)
8. Morvan 71, Footnote 29, Chapter 2
9. 'Jeanne de Clisson, The Lioness of Britanny: The Hundred Years War', 4 December 2021
10. Note: In March 1343, Olivier was again in Vannes, which was besieged by the Anglo-Breton troops commanded by the King of England in person. Olivier made an exit to push back the enemy. Argentre, B., The *History of Brittany, of the Roys, Dukes, Counts and Princes of Nicelle*, Rennes, France, 1583, p.288. During the engagement, he was taken prisoner with Herve de Leon. Le Bel, J., *Chroniques*, op cit, Chapter LCII, p.21
11. Labat-Poussin, Brigitte, Langlois, Monique and Lanhers, Yvonne, 'Reign of Philippe 6 de Valois', *Journal: Acts of the Parliament of Paris, Criminal Parliament*, Arche. Nat. X2A4, Number 4097 G., Analytical Inventory of Registers X2A to 5, Paris, 1987, p.177
12. Cazelles, R., 'Political Society and the Crisis of Royalty under Philippe VI Valois', Paris, 1958
13. Milly, David Reverchon, '*Quand l'outil devient jouet, alors le travail devient un jeu*'
14. French Arch-Nat. Reg. X 2 a 4; f. 209 v

15. *The Law of Treason and Treason Trials in Later Medieval France, (Cambridge Studies in Medieval Life and Thought)*, Third Series, 18 December 2003
16. Ibid
17. The Online Froissart, http://www.hrionline.ac.uk. Archived from the original on 1 December 2017
18. Cazelles, Raymond, *La société politique et la crise de la royauté sous Philippe de Valois (Political Society and the Crisis of Royalty Under Philippe VI Valois)*, Librairie d'Argences, Paris, France, 1958
19. Duncombe, Laura, Pirate Women: *The Princesses, Prostitutes, and Privateers Who Ruled the Seven Seas*, Chicago Review Press, Chicago, United States of America, 2017
20. Ibid
21. Vencel, Wendy, 'Undergraduate Honors Thesis Collection', 1 January 2018
22. Heebøll-Holm, Thomas, K. *Ports, Piracy and Maritime War: Piracy in the English Channel and the Atlantic,* c.*1280*–c.*1330 (Medieval Law and Its Practice)*, Brill, Netherlands, 2013
23. Cassard, Jean-Christophe, *Les Bretons et la mer as Moyen Age*, Presses Universitaires de Rennes, Rennes, France, 1998, p.152
24. Alvarez, S. *Ships and Fleets in Anglo-French Warfare, 1337–1360*, De Re Militari: The Society for Medieval Military Historians, https://deremilitari.org, 2014
25. Esseul, Maurice, *The Castle of the Island of Yeu*, Fromentine, 1980
26. Jones, Michael C.E., 'Les capitaines Anglo-Bretonz, 365–369' and 'Edward the 3rd, Captains in Brittany', *Between France and England: Politics, Power and Society in Late Medieval Brittany*, Brulington VT, Ashgate, London, 2003, p.100
27. History of War, 'Battle of Mauron', Britanny, France, 14 August 1352, https://www.historyofwar.org
28. Wagner, B.B., *Be My Matelotage! The Civil Union of 17th Century Pirates*, 2006, p.51
29. Bock, Freiderich, *Some New Documents Illustrating the Early Years of the Hundred Years' War, 1353–1356*, John Rylands Library, University of Manchester, Manchester, https://escholar.manchester.ac.uk
30. Britannica, https://www.britannica.com/event/*Black-Death*/Cause-and-outbreak
31. Wagner, J.A., *Encyclopedia of the Hundred Years' War*, Greenwood Press, Westport, Connecticut, United States of America, 2006

Bibliography

Archives

Jamaica National Archives, Jamaica
The National Archives, Kew

Articles

Cazelles, R., 'Political Society and the Crisis of Royalty under Philippe VI Valois', Paris, 1958

French Arch-Nat. Reg. X 2 a 4; f. 209 v

Hajdu, R. 'Family and Feudal Ties in Poitou, 1100–1300', *The Journal of Interdisciplinary History*, Volume 8, Number 1, summer 1977,

'Jeanne de Clisson, The Lioness of Britanny: The Hundred Years War', 4 December 2021

Jones, Michael C.E., 'Les capitaines Anglo-Bretonz, 365–369' and 'Edward the 3rd, Captains in Brittany', *Between France and England: Politics, Power and Society in Late Medieval Brittany*, Brulington VT, Ashgate, London, 2003

Labat-Poussin, Brigitte, Langlois, Monique and Lanhers, Yvonne, 'Reign of Philippe 6 de Valois', *Journal: Acts of the Parliament of Paris, Criminal Parliament*, Arche. Nat. X2A4, Number 4097 G., Analytical Inventory of Registers X2A to 5, Paris, 1987

Library of Congress Global Gateway, *King's Daughters, Casket Girls, Prostitutes*

Milly, David Reverchon, '*Quand l'outil devient jouet, alors le travail devient un jeu*'

Mollat, G., Vatican Register, Number II

Mollat G., Vatican Register, Number 95, Lettres commune 81

Mollat G., Vatican Register, John XXII, 1316–1334

Mollat, G., Vatican Register, 1921–1947

Morvan, 71, Footnote 29, Chapter 2

Murray, Theresa D., 'Early Modern History (1500–1700)', Issue 2, Volume 13, March–April 2005

Ryzhov, Valery, *Filibusters and Corsairs*, 'Top War' article, 30 July 2018

Vencel, Wendy, 'Undergraduate Honors Thesis Collection', 1 January 2018

Books

Altuntaş, Leman, *Queen of the Seas who Challenged Rome: 'Queen Teuta'*, Arkeonews, 2023

Alvarez, S. *Ships and Fleets in Anglo-French Warfare, 1337–1360*, De Re Militari: The Society for Medieval Military Historians, 2014

Andrew, Elizabeth Wheeler and Bushnell, Katharine Caroline, *Heathen Slaves and Christian Rulers, Echo Library*, 2006

Annals of Kinsale: The Council Book of the Corporation of Kinsale, From 1652 to 1800

Anthologia Hibernica, Volume II

Argentre, B., The *History of Brittany, of the Roys, Dukes, Counts and Princes of Nicelle*, Rennes, France, 1583

Boardman, John, Edwards, I.E.S., Hammond; N.G.L. and Sollberger, E. (eds.), *The Cambridge Ancient History: The Prehistory of the*

Balkans, the Middle East and the Aegean World, Tenth to Eighth Centuries BC, Vol. III, Part 1, Second Edition, Cambridge University Press, Cambridge, 1982

Bock, Freiderich, *Some New Documents Illustrating the Early Years of the Hundred Years' War, 1353–1356*, John Rylands Library, University of Manchester, Manchester

Buffé, Marcel, *Châteaubriant, une cité dans l'histoire: De la préhistoire à nos jours*, Éditions Cid, 1983

Burg, B.R., *Sodomy and the Pirate Tradition: English Sea Rovers in the Seventeenth-Century Caribbean*, second edition, New York,

University Press, New York, United States of America, 2005

Cambridge University Press, *Dictionary of Irish Biography*, Cambridge University Press, Cambridge, 2010

Captivating History, *The Golden Age of Piracy: A Captivating History to the Role of Pirates in Maritime History During the Early Modern Period,*

Including Stories of Anne Bonny, Sir Francis Drake and William Kidd (Early Modern History), Captivating History, 2021

Cassard, Jean-Christophe, *Les Bretons et la mer as Moyen Age*, Presses Universitaires de Rennes, Rennes, France, 1998

Cawthorne, Nigel, *A History of Pirates: Blood and Thunder on the High Seas*, Arcturus Publishing, London, 2003

Cawthorne, Nigel, *A History of Pirates, Blood and Thunder on the High Seas*, Capella, United States of America, 2003

Cazelles, Raymond, *La société politique et la crise de la royauté sous Philippe de Valois (Political Society and the Crisis of Royalty Under Philippe VI Valois)*, Librairie d'Argences, Paris, France, 1958

Cole, Bernard D., *The Great Wall at Sea: China's Navy in the Twenty-First*

Century, Naval Institute Press, Annapolis, United States of America, 2010

Cordingly, David, *Pirates: An Illustrated History of Privateers, Buccaneers & Pirates from the Sixteenth Century to the Present, Salamander Books Limited, London, 1996 (Book referenced History of Pirates of All Nations, 1836)*

Cordingly, David, *Seafaring Women: Adventures of Pirate Queens, Female Stowaways, and Sailors' Wives*, Random House, Trade paperback edition, New York, 2007

Coulon, A. and Clemencet, S., *Lettres Secretes et Curiales*, Jean XXII (1316–1334)

de Palafox y Mendoza, Juan, *Diálogo político del estado de Alemania*, Spain, 1632?

de Palafox y Mendoza, Juan, *Dialogo político del estado de Alemania y comparación de España con las demás naciones*, More Than Books, 'Clasicos Hispánicos', Madrid, Spain, 2015

Duncombe, Laura Snook, *Pirate Women: The Princesses, Prostitutes, and Privateers Who Ruled the Seven Seas*, Chicago Review Press, Chicago, United States of America, 2017

Elgenstierna, G. and Ättartavlor, Svenska Adelns, *Index to Muster Rolls*, Volume 7, Swedish Krigsarkiv, Stockholm, Sweden, 1864

Emerson Kathy Lynn, *A Who's Who of Tudor Women*, Kathy Lynn Emerson, 2020

Esseul, Maurice, *The Castle of the Island of Yeu*, Fromentine, 1980

Exquemelin, Alexander, *De Americanensche Zee-Roovers* (American Sea Rovers also known as Buccaneers of America), Amsterdam, 1678

Fryxell, Anders, *Berättelser ur svenska historien*, Sweden, 1846

Goude, Charles, *Histoire de Châteaubriant. Baronnie, Ville et Paroisse*, Oberthur et fils, Rennes, France, 1870

Hajdu, R. 'Family and Feudal Ties in Poitou, 1100–1300', *The Journal of Interdisciplinary History*, Volume 8, Number 1, summer 1977

Heebøll-Holm, Thomas, K. *Ports, Piracy and Maritime War: Piracy in the English Channel and the Atlantic,* c.*1280*–c.*1330 (Medieval Law and Its Practice)*, Brill, Netherlands, 2013

Grimau, Rodolfo Gil (Benumeya), '*Sayyida al-Hurra, Mujer Marroquí de Origen Andalusí*', *Anaquel de Estudios Árabes*, 11:311, January 2000

Heidelberg University, Po, Chung-yam, *Conceptualizing the Blue Frontier*, https://archiv.ub.uni-heidelberg.de/volltextserver/18877/1/PhD_Dissertation_CyPO.pdf

Histoire General des Antilles, Volume 1, 1667

History of Pirates of All Nations,1836

Jamaica National Archives, *The Tryals of Captain John Rackham and Others*, 1721

Johnson, Captain Charles (also known as Defoe, Daniel), *A General History of Pyrates*, 1724

Johnson, Captain Charles (also known as Defoe, Daniel), *A General History of the Robberies and Murders of the Most Notorious Pyrates*, 1724

Jones, Michael C.E., 'Les capitaines Anglo-Bretonz, 365–369' and 'Edward the 3rd, Captains in Brittany', *Between France and England: Politics, Power and Society in Late Medieval Brittany*, Brulington VT, Ashgate, London, 2003

Kvinnor, Svenska Män och, *Anteckningar om Svenska Qvinnor*, Volume 7, Stockholm, Sweden,1864

Kretschmer, P., *Einleitung in die Geschichte der Griechischen Sprachen*, Göttingen, 1896

Labat-Poussin, Brigitte, Langlois, Monique and Lanhers, Yvonne, 'Reign of Philippe 6 de Valois', *Journal: Acts of the Parliament of Paris, Criminal Parliament*, Arche. Nat. X2A4, Number 4097 G., Analytical Inventory of Registers X2A to 5, Paris, 1987

Le Bel, J., *Chroniques*

Memissi, Fatima, *The Forgotten Queens of Islam*, University of Minnesota Press, Minnesota, United States of America, 1997

Murray, Dian H., Pirates of the South China Coast, 1790–1810, Stanford University Press, Stanford, California, United States of America, 1987, pp.71, 143

Neumann, Charles Fried, *The History of Pirates Who Infested the China Sea: From 1807 to 1810*, Fb&c Limited, 2017

Owen, Erika, Wright, Alexander (Illustrator), *Lawbreaking Ladies: 50 Tales of Daring, Defiant, and Dangerous Women from History*, S&S/Simon Element, United States of America, 2021, pp.6–7

Parker, Charles H., *Global Interactions in the Early Modern Age, 1400–1800*, Cambridge University Press, Cambridge, 2010

Parkinson, William A. (editor), *The Archaeology of Tribal Societies*, 'Modeling [*sic*] the Evolution and Formation of an Illyrian Tribal System' by Galaty, Michael L., Berghahn Books, New York, United States of America, 2002

Pierre, Margry, *Relations et Mémoires Inédits pour Servir à L'histoire de la France sous les Pays D'outre-mer Tirés des Archives du Ministère de la Marine et des Colonies, Challamel*, 1867

Po, Chung-yam, Heidelberg University, *Conceptualizing the Blue Frontier*, https://archiv.ub.uni-heidelberg.de/volltextserver/18877/1/PhD_Dissertation_CyPO.pdf

Polybius and Shuckburgh, E. (translator), *Histories*, Book 2, Number 2, MacMillan, London, 1889

Polybius and Shuckburgh, E. (translator), *Histories*, Book 2, Number 5, MacMillan, London, 1889

Polybius and Shuckburgh, E. (translator), *Histories*, Book 2, Number 7, MacMillan, London, 1889

Polybius and Shuckburgh, E. (translator), *Histories*, Book 2, Number 8, MacMillan, London, 1889

Polybius and Shuckburgh, E. (translator), *Histories*, Book 2, Number 9, MacMillan, London, 1889

Polybius and Shuckburgh, E. (translator), *Histories*, Book 2, Number 10, MacMillan, London, 1889

Polybius and Shuckburgh, E. (translator), *Histories*, Book 2, Number 11, MacMillan, London, 1889

Seymour, *Jean-Jacques, Les Chemins des Proies: une Histoire de la Flibuste, Ibis Rouge Éd.*, 2010

Sharp, Anne Wallace, *Daring Pirate Women*, Lerner Publications, United States, 2002

Strabo, *Geographica*, Volume I, 7 BCE (last printed during his lifetime in 23 CE)

Sumption, Jonathan, *The Hundred Years' War*, The MIT Press, Massachusetts, United States of America

Sumption, Jonathan, *The Hundred Years' War: Trial by Battle*, Volume 1, Faber and Faber, London, 1990

Swartz, Stuart B., *Copper Dreams and the 'Hope of the North.' Sweden, Portugal and Spain During the Portuguese Rebellion, 1640–1668*

Part I, Politika

Sylvander, Gustaf Volmar, *Kalmar stads och slotts historia*, Sweden, 1865

The Great Qing and the Maritime World in the Long Eighteenth Century

The Law of Treason and Treason Trials in Later Medieval France, (Cambridge Studies in Medieval Life and Thought), Third Series, 18 December 2003

Thornbury, Walter, *Monarchs of the Main*, 1861

Wagner, B.B., *Be My Matelotage! The Civil Union of 17th Century Pirates*, 2006

Wagner, J.A., *Encyclopedia of the Hundred Years' War*, Greenwood Press, Westport, Connecticut, United States of America, 2006

Wilkes, John, *The Illyrians*, Wiley-Blackwell, United States, 1992

Woodard, Colin, *The Republic of Pirates Being the True and Surprising Story of the Caribbean Pirates and The Man Who Brought Them Down*, Harcourt, United States of America, 2007

Ye, Lingfeng, 张保仔的传说和真相, *The Myths and Truths of Zhang Bao the Kid, Nanchang, Jiangx,* 江西教育出版社, *2012*

Images

The author has endeavoured to locate all copyright holders and provide proper acknowledgments for material included in this book that is not her own. However, if a credit to any copyrighter holder has been omitted, please make yourself known to the publisher so that this may be corrected in any reprint or future edition.

Films

Pirates of the Caribbean

Magazines

LBV Independent Magazine of Culture, Alvarez, Jorge, *The Chinese Woman Who Became Queen of Piracy with a Fleet of Hundreds of Ships*, 2020

Wreckwatch

Museums

Sörmlands Museum, 'Anna Christina Skytte'

Newspapers

Daily Mail

Notes

Note: On 10 February 1330, in Avignon, France, at the request of Guy de Bretagne, Pope Jean XXII appointed the bishops of Rennes and Vannes to investigate the alleged marriage that was supposedly contracted in 1328 by Jeanne de Belleville, widow of the Lord of Chateaubriant, and Guy de Bretagne, seigneur de Penthievre. Mollat, G., op cit, pj, Number II pp.49–50. See also Jean XXII (1316–1334) *Lettres Secretes et Curiales* relating to France by Coulon, A. and Clemencet, S. If Jeanne could not deny Guy's words. Guy could remarry. Mollat, G. op cit, p.47. A little later, on 30 April 1330, Jeanne de Belleville, widow of Geoffroy de Chateaubriant, asked the Holy See for a dispensation to marry Olivier de Clisson. Mollat, G. op cit, p.47, after Vatican Register, Number 95, Lettres commune 81. See John XXII (1316–1334). Joint letters analysed according to the so-called Avignon or Vatican registers by Mollat, G. (1921–1947)

Note: In March 1343, Olivier was again in Vannes, which was besieged by the Anglo-Breton troops commanded by the King of England in person. Olivier made an exit to push back the enemy. Argentre, B., The *History of Brittany, of the Roys, Dukes, Counts and Princes of Nicelle*, Rennes, France, 1583, p.288. During the engagement, he was taken prisoner with Herve de Leon. Le Bel, J., *Chroniques*, op cit, Chapter LCII, p.21

Television Series

Black Sails

Thesis

Smith, Emily, *Never the Twain Shall Part: A Comparison and Analysis of Irish and English Marriage Laws Following the English Conquest of Ireland*, Masters Thesis, 2010

Websites

Adelsvapen, https://www.adelsvapen.com/genealogi/Skytte_af_Duderhof_nr_8

Alvarez, S. *Ships and Fleets in Anglo-French Warfare, 1337–1360*, De Re Militari: The Society for Medieval Military Historians, https://deremilitari.org, 2014

Amirell, Stefan Eklöf, 'Christina Anna Skytte', (article by Amirell, Stefan Eklöf) retrieved 27 August 2024, Svenskt kvinnobiografiskt lexikon, https://www.skbl.se/sv/artikel/AnnaSkytte

Ancient Origins, Wagner, B.B., *Be My Matelotage! The Civil Union of 17th Century Pirates*, 2006, Ancient Origins, https://www.ancient-origins.net/history-ancient-traditions/matelotage-0012504

AramcoWorld, Verde, Tom, *Malika* (Queen), January/February 2017 and Special Edition, 2021, https://www.aramcoworld.com/Articles/January-2017/Malika-VI-Sayyida-Al-Hurra

Atlas Obscura, Banerji, Urvija, *Ching Shih, Who Lived and Pillaged During the Qing Dynasty, Has Been Called the Most Successful Pirate in History*, https://www.atlasobscura.com/articles/ching-shih-chinese-female-pirate

Banerji, Urvija, *Ching Shih, Who Lived and Pillaged During the Qing Dynasty, Has Been Called the Most Successful Pirate in History*, Atlas Obscura, https://www.atlasobscura.com/articles/ching-shih-chinese-female-pirate

Bock, Freiderich, *Some New Documents Illustrating the Early Years of the Hundred Years' War, 1353–1356*, John Rylands Library, University of Manchester, Manchester, https://escholar.manchester.ac.uk

Bone, Katherine, *The History of Maritime Piracy Pirates and Privateers*, Pirates and Privateers: The History of Maritime Piracy, (Cindy Vallar, Editor and Reviewer), http//www.cindyvallar.com/Tortuga.html

Britannica, https://www.britannica.com/event/Black-Death/Cause-and-outbreakBruyneel, Mark, *A Short History of Tortuga, 1625–1688*, Isle of Tortuga, http://zeerovery.nl/history/tortuga.html

Cambridge University Press, https://dib.cambridge.org

Collins, Dr A.R., *British Cannon Design (1600–1800)*, Miscellany, https://www.arc.id.au

Cornish Bird Blog, https://cornishbirdblog.com/the-notorious-women-of-the-killigrew-family/

Cunliffe, Ciaran, *Cheung Po Tsai and Ching Shih: Pirate Monarchs*, Head Stuff, https://headstuff.org/culture/history/ching-shih-and-cheung-po-tsai-pirate-monarchs/

Daily Mail, https://www.dailymail.co.uk/news/article-13708787/Controversial-treasure-hunters-discovered-pirate-shipwreck.html

De Re Militari: The Society for Medieval Military Historians, Alvarez, S. *Ships and Fleets in Anglo-French Warfare, 1337–1360*, https://deremilitari.org, 2014

Exploring Celtic Civilizations, *Exploring Celtic Civilizations*,

https://exploringcelticciv.web.unc.edu/1537-act-for-the-english-order-habit-and-language

Exquemelin, Alexander, Library of Congress

https://www.loc.gov/exhibits/exploring-the-early-americas/interactives/buccaneers-of-america/

Frith, John, *Syphilis: Its Early History and Treatment Until Penicillin and the Debate on its Origins*, JVMH Volume 20, Number 4, Journal of Military and Veterans History

Gaelta, https://gaelta.ie/Gráinne-omalley-the-pirate-queen

Geni, https://www.geni.com/photo/view/6000000001531288646?album type=photos_of_me&photo_id=6000000123708026865

Geni, https://www.geni.com/people/Capt-John-Killigrew/6000000001531288654

Geni, https://www.geni.com/people/Geoffroy-VIII-de-Ch%C3%A2teaubriant/6000000013087519492Geni, https://www.geni.com/people/Lady-Elizabeth Killigrew/6000000001531288646

Grace O'Malley, Anne Chambers, https://www.graceomalley-annechambers.com

Gráinne O'Malley, https://www.dib.ie/biography/omalley-Gráinne-grace-granuaile-a6886

Head Stuff, https://headstuff.org/culture/history/ching-shih-and-cheung-po-tsai-pirate-monarchs/

History of Parliament, https://www.historyofparliamentonline.org/volume/1558-1603/member/killigrew-john-i-1584

Historic UK, https://www.historicuk.com

History of War, 'Battle of Mauron', Britanny, France, 14 August 1352, https://www.historyofwar.org

Internet Archives, https://ia904607.us.archive.org/17/items/monarchsofmain00thorrich/monarchsofmain00thorrich.pdfIsle of Tortuga, http://zeerovery.nl/history/tortuga.html

James Ford Bell Library, online exhibitions and instructional resources, *Anne Bonny Early Life*, https://gallcry.lib.umn.edu/exhibits/show/mary-read-anne-bonny/anne-bonny/anne-bonny--early life

John Rylands Library, Bock, Freiderich, *Some New Documents Illustrating the Early Years of the Hundred Years' War, 1353–1356*, John Rylands

Library, University of Manchester, Manchester, https://escholar.manchester.ac.uk

Library of Congress, https://www.loc.gov/exhibits/exploring-the-early-americas/interactives/buccaneers-of-america/

Miscellany, https://www.arc.id.au

Munro, Sophie, *Anne Bonny 1690–1778*, 2 March 2017, https://womenshistorynetwork.org/anne-bonny-c-1690-c-1778

Murdoch, Steve and Grosjean, Alexia, University of St Andrews, Institute of Scottish Historical Research, FORRAT, MARGAREHTA (SSNE 6267), University of St Andrews, https://www.st-andrews.ac.uk/history/ssne/item.php?id=6267

Murdoch, Steve and Grosjean, Alexia, University of St Andrews, Institute of Scottish Historical Research, HAMILTON, BRITA MARGARETHA (SSNE 6386), University of St Andrews, https://www.st-andrews.ac.uk/ history/ssne/item.php?id=6386

Murdoch, Steve and Grosjean, Alexia, University of St Andrews, Institute of Scottish Historical Research, HAMILTON, HUGH (SSNE 2582), University of St Andrews, https://www.st-andrews.ac.uk/history/ssne/item.php?id=2582

Murdoch, Steve and Grosjean, Alexia, University of St Andrews, Institute of Scottish Historical Research, SKYTTE, GUSTAV ADOLF (SSNE 4921), University of St Andrews, https://www.st-andrews.ac.uk/history/ssne/item.php?id=4921

New Historian, https://www.newhistorian.com/wp-content/uploads/2018/07/Ching-Shih-1-1.jpgPirates and Privateers: The History of Maritime Piracy, (Cindy Vallar, Editor and Reviewer), http//www.cindyvallar.com/Tortuga.html

Portrait to a Lady, https://portraitoalady.blogspot.com/2020/06/01-painting-portrait-of-lady-with_24.html

Rikarkivet (in Swedish/translated from Swedish Gustaf Drake Biografi), https://sok.riksarkivet.se/sbl/Presentation.aspx?id=17630

Seymour, *Jean-Jacques, Les Chemins des Proies: une Histoire de la Flibuste, Ibis Rouge Éd.*, 2010

Share Ok, https://shareok.org/bitstream/handle/11244/9085/

Smith_okstate_0664M_10808.pdf?sequence=1&isAllowed=y

Smith, Amy, *Meet Ching Shih: The Prostitute-Turned-Pirate Who Banned Rape in Her 50,000-Man Fleet*, 25 July 2018, New Historian, https://www.newhistorian.com/wp-content/uploads/2018/07/Ching-Shih-1-1.jpg

Stewart, Terry, The South Seas Bubble, https://www.historicuk.com/ HistoryUK/HistoryofEngland/South-Sea-Bubble

Svenskt kvinnobiografiskt lexicon, Amirell, Stefan Eklöf, 'Christina Anna Skytte', (article by Amirell, Stefan Eklöf) retrieved 27 August 2024, https://www.skbl.se/sv/artikel/AnnaSkytte

The Canton System, https://en.wikipedia.org/wiki/Canton_System

The LeEms Machine, *The Legend of Jacquotte Delahaye*, https://theleemsmachine.com/bean/blog/2022/01/12/the-legend-of-jacquotte-delahaye/

The Online Froissart, http://www.hrionline.ac.uk

Thornbury, Walter, *Monarchs of the Main*, London, 1861, Chapter 1, p.B2., US Archives, https://ia904607.us.archive.org/17/items/monarchsofmain00thorrich/monarchsofmain00thorrich.pdf

University of Manchester, John Rylands Library, Bock, Freiderich, *Some New Documents Illustrating the Early Years of the Hundred Years' War, 1353–1356*, John Rylands Library, University of Manchester, Manchester, https://escholar.manchester.ac.uk

University of St Andrew's, https://www.st-andrews.ac.uk/history/ssne/

University of St Andrews, Murdoch, Steve and Grosjean, Alexia, Institute of Scottish Historical Research, FORRAT, MARGAREHTA (SSNE 6267), University of St Andrews, https://www.st-andrews.ac.uk/history/ssne/item.php?id=6267

University of St Andrews, Murdoch, Steve and Grosjean, Alexia, Institute of Scottish Historical Research, HAMILTON, BRITA MARGARETHA (SSNE 6386), University of St Andrews, https://www.st-andrews.ac.uk/history/ssne/item.php?id=6386

University of St Andrews, Murdoch, Steve and Grosjean, Alexia, Institute of Scottish Historical Research, HAMILTON, HUGH (SSNE 2582), University of St Andrews, https://www.st-andrews.ac.uk/history/ssne/item.php?id=2582

University of St Andrews, Murdoch, Steve and Grosjean, Alexia, Institute of Scottish Historical Research, SKYTTE, GUSTAV ADOLF (SSNE 4921), University of St Andrews, https://www.st-andrews.ac.uk/history/ssne/item.php?id=4921

Vallar, Cindy (Editor and Reviewer – Pirates and Privateers: The History of Maritime Piracy), http//www.cindyvallar.com/Tortuga.html

Vendeens Archives, http://vendeens-archives.vendee.fr

Verde, Tom, *Malika* (Queen), January/February 2017 and Special Edition, 2021, AramcoWorld, https://www.aramcoworld.com/Articles/January-2017/Malika-VI-Sayyida-Al-Hurra

Wagner, B.B., *Be My Matelotage! The Civil Union of 17th Century Pirates*, 2006, Ancient Origins, https://www.ancient-origins.net/history-ancient-traditions/matelotage-0012504

Wikipedia, https://commons.wikimedia.org/wiki/File:Illyrians_in_the_1st-2nd_centuries_CE.png

Wikipedia, https://commons.wikimedia.org/wiki/File:Pendennis_Castle.jpg

Wikipedia, https://en.wikipedia.org

Wikipedia, https://en.wikipedia.org/wiki/Anne_Bonny#/media/File:Ann_Bonny_December_29_1733.png

Wikipedia, *The Battle of Tiger Mouth*, https://en.wikipedia.org/wiki/Battle_of_the_Tiger%27s_Mouth

Wikipedia, https://en.wikipedia.org/wiki/DanoSwedish_War_(1657%E2%80%931658)

Wikipedia, https://en.wikipedia.org/wiki/Device_Forts

Wikipedia, https://en.wikipedia.org/wiki/Laurens_de_Graaf#/media/File:Graff_Lorens.jpg

Wikipedia, https://en.wikipedia.org/wiki/Maria_Skytte https://en.wikipedia.org/wiki/Mary_Wolverston

Wikipedia, https://en.wikipedia.org/wiki/Mary_Wolverston#cite_note-AWS-8

Wikipedia, https://en.wikipedia.org/wiki/South_Sea_Company

Wikipedia, https://en.wikipedia.org/wiki/Tartane#/media/File:Tartane.gif

Wikipedia, https://en.wikipedia.org/wiki/Women _in_piracy

Wikipedia, https://en.wikipedia.org/wiki/Zheng_Yi_(pirate)

Wikipedia, https://en.wikipedia.org/wiki/Zheng_Yi_Sao

Wikipedia, https://en.wikipedia.org/wiki/Zheng_Yi_Sao#CITEREFYe2012

Wikipedia, https://upload.wikimedia.org/wikipedia/commons/9/9e/FortRoche-381-59.jpg

Wikipedia, image of Gráinne O'Malley, 1530–1603, the Irish Pirate, located at Westport House, County Mayo, Ireland

Wise Money Rum, https://wisemonkeyrum.com/blog/rum-and-gunpowder-the-cocktail-favoured-by-the-bold

Women's History Network, https://womenshistorynetwork.org/anne-bonny-c-1690-c-1778

Yvan, Melchoir, *Inside Canton*, Henry Vizetelly, Gough Square, London, 1858

Zeerovery, Isle of Tortuga, http://zeerovery.nl/history/tortuga.html

Zuidhoek, Arne, *Heet Nel Cuyper: Avonturierster van Oudewater; een biografie (Lady Pirates)*, Utrecht, 2019

Index